Believe to Achieve

The Power of Perseverance

A personal story of adversity, aspirations and purpose.

By

Lynn Effinger

Cover Photo: Carl Kravats Photography

Copyright © 2011. Lynn Effinger.
All rights reserved.
ISBN - 0615470688
ISBN - 13: 9780615470689
LCCN: 2011905443

Dedicated with deep love, affection and gratitude to my beautiful wife of more than 40 years, Kathy, for her unyielding support, undying love, and unilateral forgiveness.

Contents

Foreword		ix
Introduction		xi
Preface		xv
1.	Growing Up "Different"	1
2.	Baseball Fever	19
3.	The Center-Fielder of Attention	43
4.	New Challenges	53
5.	Learning to Apply the *Power* of Perseverance	69
6.	The Year of the Underdog	87
7.	A Cinderella Team…Time to Be Bold	99
8.	My "Responsibility"	127
9.	College, Marriage, and More	139
10.	The "Impossible" Dream?	159
11.	A Dream Come True	183
12.	Getting Down to Business	199
13.	A Roller Coaster Existence	219
14.	The Journey Continues	235
15.	More Opportunities…Marching On	251
16.	Tenacity Matters	271
Afterword		297
Acknowledgements		299
About the Author		305

What People Have Said:

"It is truly heartening to know that you are inspiring others. It seems my father's blood and especially his spirit is continuing through your dedicated, motivational leadership and example."
— The Honorable George Allen, Former Governor and Senator of Virginia (from a personal letter, with permission)

"I appreciate more than you can know your taking the time to share so much of your story with me. It's an exciting story, Lynn, and I believe as you do that it can be an inspiration and encouragement to many people."
— Zig Ziglar, Author and Motivational Teacher (from a personal letter, with permission)

"Enjoyed greatly reading your book about growing up 'Different.' It brought back memories of my 35 years at Wilson. I am very pleased to {read} about your family, career, successes and all the things that made you a CHAMPION."
— Gene "Skip" Rowland, Retired Teacher, Coach and Icon at Long Beach Woodrow Wilson High School

"A book about the power of perseverance is completely appropriate from Lynn Effinger. Whether it is in his personal life, his business career or in the world of sports, Lynn has always believed in his ability to achieve no matter what challenges have been thrown his way. We are all lucky to learn from him in this excellent book."
— George Chamberlin, Executive Editor, San Diego Daily Transcript

"... all my best to an inspiration not only to young men and women everywhere but to an old NFL quarterback."
  – The Honorable Jack Kemp, Former Congressman, HUD Secretary and Vice Presidential Candidate

"Lynn Effinger is the most dynamic, inspirational and stimulating speaker in the mortgage default servicing industry,"
  – Shelley Kaye, Executive Director of Women in Default Services

Foreword

IT IS WITH GREAT EXCITEMENT and pleasure that I have the opportunity to introduce you to my friend and colleague Lynn Effinger. Lynn is one of those unique individuals who exemplify perseverance. He has lived his life never backing away from any challenge and proving to all that accomplishments are a matter of decision and determination. If you are around Lynn for just a few minutes, you will soon learn of the passion that pours out from his heart, always wanting to impact the lives of others by encouraging them to "go for it." I am invigorated by Lynn's desire and mission to help others overcome adversity. Like so many others I have been drawn to Lynn because we can all relate to adversity in our own lives.

The book, *Believe to Achieve - The Power of Perseverance,* is an amazing story of the reality and brutality of our fallen world and how a young man finds himself and perseveres amidst many challenges and doubters. I wish every child could grow up with the same confidence that they are a unique, special creation. Lynn figured that out and now attacks life as an opportunity to make a difference. I am reminded of the first time I met Lynn in a crowded room of people listening to him and several other panelists offering economic insight. Lynn's comments came from a real and passionate place into which I was immediately drawn. *Believe To Achieve – The Power of Perseverance* will touch, encourage and challenge you to approach life with an improved attitude and perspective.

I have also had the pleasure of sharing the stage with Lynn at a real estate industry-related trade-association meeting recently in Orange County, California. His command of an audience and enthusiasm for delivering his powerful message is inspiring, indeed. His desire to reach a wider audience to better fulfill his stated purpose in life was the driving force behind his authorship of this moving memoir. I am honored that Lynn asked me to pen this Foreword and to play a part in his mission to help others learn to overcome adversity to be the best they can be.

–**Matt Luke**
–Motivational Speaker and Former
Major League Baseball Player

Introduction

My son Lynn, the second of our four children, has given me the distinct honor of writing this introduction to his unique and compelling autobiography. Character, above all is what Lynn's story exhibits. Having the inner strength to overcome the odds and the naysayers of the world to achieve his dreams is his most important achievement and the message this book delivers.

Lynn is not the subject of his book; he is the metaphor for showing us that in order to overcome adversity, whether physical or mental, maintaining the right attitude is paramount. He set out to prove this to us all. He has accomplished his goals mostly on his own while we have proudly watched from the sidelines. He shares many of his innermost thoughts from his earliest memories as a child. In so doing, he has bravely laid open for us his most closely held and guarded moments of hurt, growing up "different"; Things as his father I feared from the very day he was born when I first kissed him and his mother as we shed a few tears together.

As parents, we only get to see and share experiences with the outer self of our children, interacting with them as they grow into adults; in those rare moments when they might confide a fear or doubt. Lynn was never a "talker" but always a "doer" with an independent streak. He was determined to make his own way. Most often he declined help from others and rarely took the "easy way" to accomplish his goals, whatever they may have been.

Much of Lynn's inner thoughts that you will read in this autobiography I have learned for the first time, having wanted to know, but too afraid to ask. Not being brave enough to risk asking him the question of how he was feeling about himself may not be a testament for good fatherhood, but it's the truth. I could never bring myself to ask him for fear of hurting him. Reading Lynn's book has been a cathartic experience for me.

Right or wrong, we decided from the beginning of Lynn's life that we would not allow ourselves or others to coddle or patronize him in any way. We knew that growing up without a left hand was going to be a hardship for him, but we were determined not to let this keep him from doing anything he really wanted to do.

As patriarch of our growing family one of my responsibilities was to set rules. The first of those for the entire family was that the word "can't," should never be used in our home. In my view under the circumstances it was the worst four-letter word in the dictionary. I was chastised many times for this by friends and relatives, declaring that I was in denial of Lynn's "handicap," which was the second word that was not welcome in our home.

What Lynn reveals and shares with us in this book is his overriding self-determination in addressing what life has given him and what long ago, through the urging of a very introspective football coach, became his destiny to share with others.

Sports were anathema to me growing up in a blue-collar family trying to make our way during the depression. Earning enough money to eat and pay the rent was about all we had time for other than some sand-lot baseball, and skiing and skating in the winter months of Minnesota. So when Lynn's desire to play Little League Baseball was announced to us I wasn't much help, other than to work out a system of catching and throwing the ball using the same hand to do both. He and his coaches did the rest.

For me, as I read the page-turning play-by-play depiction of Lynn's and his teammates' exploits on the football field in high school, college, and semi-pro football, is like watching a slow-motion movie. I am back there in the stands or on the sidelines 45 years ago, eagerly turning the page to get to the next skirmish.

To say we as a family are proud of Lynn is an understatement of the highest order. Together we have experienced the same frustrations, disappointments, and arguments of many families; stumbling through ups and downs, making the best of any given situation. One of my favorite statements to all of our children, which over the years has become a family joke is, "it builds character" when life kicked one of the kids in the seat of the pants and they would complain.

I hope you will enjoy reading *Believe to Achieve – The Power of Perseverance* as much as I have, and that in so doing, you will apply lessons learned from within its pages to help you or your loved ones to overcome adversity to achieve your dreams and ambitions.

Proudly,
Bill Effinger

Preface

In early January of 1974 I was 23 years old. I was about to embark on an extraordinary, life-defining mission. When I set what many thought at the time was an impossible goal to achieve I didn't really envision the magnitude of the outcome of that demanding undertaking. Nor of others that would follow.

Because I had been born without a left hand I had some unique challenges growing up. They weren't drastically more difficult than those of the average child or young adult; certainly not as complex as those faced by others with much more severe physical and/or mental disabilities. But they were challenges nonetheless. Something as simple for most people as getting dressed, tying my shoes, doing chores, tying my own ties, performing manual labor, or picking up a child required "creativity." Not daunting mind you, but frustrating at times, embarrassing at others and sometimes maddening. It has been said that it is not what happens to you, but how you choose to handle what happens to you that matters most. I certainly embrace that belief.

By interacting with classmates during recess or when we were exercising in grade school playing a variety of physical games and other activities I discovered that by doing well at them I was more readily accepted by my peers. I also received no small measure of recognition and respect. This was good for my self-esteem, although I had no idea what that meant back then. I just knew I felt good about myself. Additionally, the praise I received from my parents, close relatives, teachers and others fueled my desire to receive more of the same. Earning self-esteem and self-respect through positive acknowledgements have ever since meant far more to me than any monetary rewards ever could. Perhaps because I learned that they are not entitlements.

Having a good sense of humor, sometimes at my own expense, a creative mind and some artistic ability also garnered me mostly positive recognition. Sometimes, however, they led me afoul of the displeasure and even wrath of some teachers who didn't appreciate my status as class clown or resident artist. But overall my experiences while growing up prepared me well for bigger challenges ahead. Challenges that would come to define who I am and what I can achieve.

On that special day in January of 1974 I had picked up a copy of our local newspaper, the *Long Beach Independent Press-Telegram*. On the front page of the Sports Section was a big photo and accompanying story about Ed Giles. Eddie was a former Long Beach Poly High School star running back against whom I had played varsity football while attending Woodrow Wilson High School and alongside as a teammate at Long Beach City College. It was a very lengthy, flattering article that focused on Eddie's football career in high school and college and his recent signing as a free agent to try out for the Los Angeles Rams of the National Football League.

After finishing the article I said to my wife, Kathy that I thought it was great that Eddie was getting a shot at the pros. But I also told her that I thought that although he was a very good running back, he really wasn't that much better than I had been. Statistically, I was a bit disingenuous, to say the least. But to my ego and my strong belief in myself and my abilities I was always better than history might substantiate. Suddenly, as if a light bulb had gone off over my head, I had an idea. I immediately realized a way that I could fulfill the "Responsibility" that one of my football coaches, Ewing H. "Bill" Crutchfield had instilled in me when I was a senior in high school. For several years thereafter I had no clue as to how to go about doing so. This responsibility and my discovery as to how I would fulfill it would evolve over time and become a driving force in all that I would accomplish over the next four decades.

The manifestation of my "light-bulb" realization was the idea to start working out in earnest to get myself into the best physical shape of my life. Then I would try out for a semi-pro football team, make the team, do well and earn a tryout with a team in the National Football League. I believed that if I could accomplish this extraordinary mission and publicize it somehow I could demonstrate to others that through hard work, discipline, determination and a burning desire to achieve success anyone can overcome adversity and persevere despite any challenges or obstacles in their path.

At the time I had a budding career in the housing industry. I was the youngest outside contractor lumber salesman for one of the largest and most successful lumber companies in California. I was married, had a three-year-old son and another child on the way. But Kathy understood my passion for setting and accomplishing this major goal. She encouraged me to do it. She supported me because I believed in myself and unabashedly believed that I would persevere to accomplish this despite the overwhelming odds against me. And because we both believed that I was compelled and destined by a power greater than myself to achieve it.

This memoire chronicles much of my life and the influential events leading up to the establishment and pursuit of my extraordinary, improbable mission, and the outcome of my most earnest efforts. It continues to explain how the principles learned in pursuit of this mission, which I call the "Golden Rules – Winning Ways to Peak Performance," were later utilized to achieve vocational successes time and time again. The intent being to demonstrate to you the reader that if I could overcome adversity to accomplish success by adhering to these principles, so can you. The book also chronicles some of the failures I experienced along the way to put things in perspective; not every goal was achieved, just the ones that meant the most to me. It has been said that you cannot experience the highest peaks unless you have also experienced the deepest valleys. I believe this to be true.

It is critically important to understand that not all of us will become hall-of-fame professional athletes, movie stars, billionaire tycoons, the number-one best there is at this or that, best-selling authors and the like. But by striving to be the best at what you choose to pursue in life you most certainly will be the best that *you* can be. Bart Starr, the great quarterback who led the Green Bay Packers to five NFL Championships and two Super Bowl victories, once said that although perfection is not attainable, by striving for perfection you will achieve excellence. That is my point.

I passionately believe that I was placed on earth to inspire and motivate others to help them learn to overcome obstacles to become the best that they can be. To achieve success as they define it. This is what I refer to as the "Golden Goal."

This tome also expresses my realization that the great mission I had pursued in 1974 was not a destination after all, but the beginning of a fascinating, rewarding, yet challenging journey that continues on to this very day.

Believe to Achieve.

– Lynn Effinger

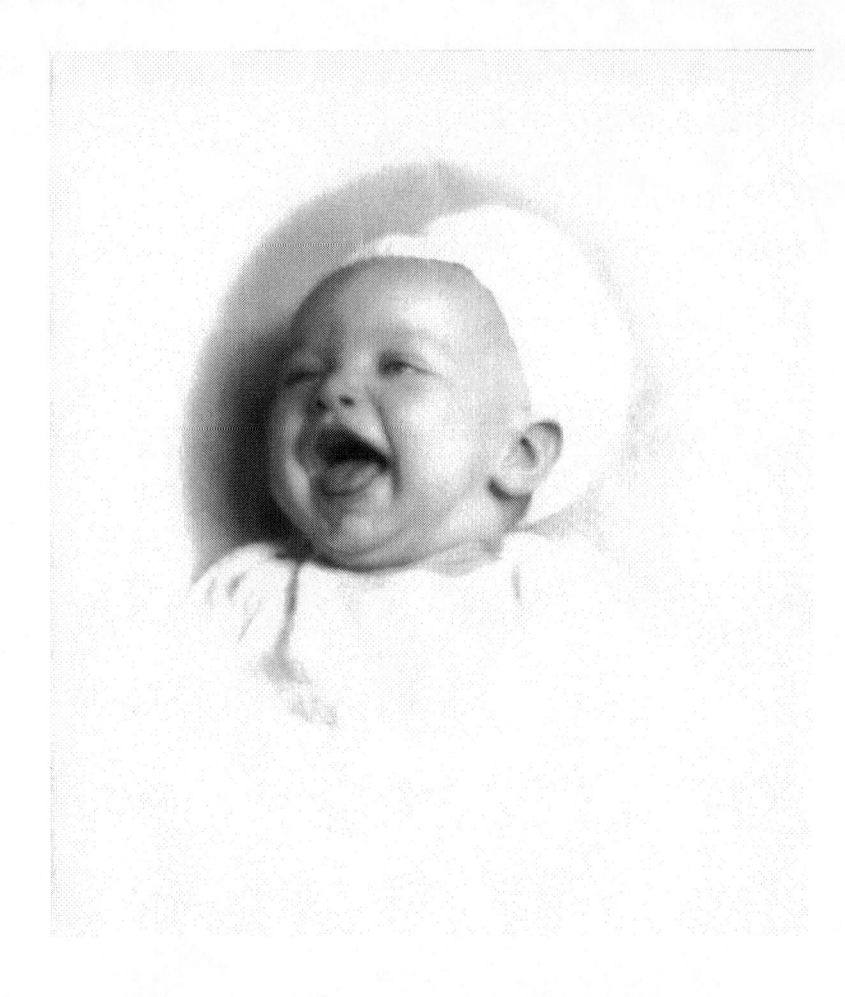

Lynn Thomas Effinger in 1951 at four months old.

Chapter One

Growing Up "Different"

"You gotta play the hand that's dealt you. There may be pain in that hand, but you play it."

– James Brady

Growing Up "Different"

WHEN I WAS GROWING UP in Southern California in the 1950s I learned pretty early that I was different. Frankly, other people made sure that I knew I was different. Having been born without a left hand, even when I was a baby my parents often had to explain to curious relatives and others what "happened" to me. My parents were happy to have a second son, but their joy was tempered by the thought that I would most likely have a difficult time growing up. They were prescient to a degree, but also underestimated my potential resolve over the years to live life to the fullest measure possible.

There was never a definitive reason or explanation given to my parents by the doctor who delivered me or anyone else as to why I didn't fully develop in the womb of my mother. She hadn't taken Thalidomide, a sedative drug introduced in the 1950s which was later discovered to cause severe birth defects in babies born to mothers who had taken the drug during pregnancy. Mom never really knew why I was born this way. Unfortunately, she early on harbored unfounded guilt thinking maybe she had done something during her pregnancy that caused my birth defect. Her feelings of guilt were groundless, of course. Nonetheless she felt how she felt.

As for my father, he told his mother one evening shortly after I had been born that he felt that maybe it was God's way of punishing him for some wrong he had done. It is perhaps understandable that he, like my mother also felt responsible. Eventually, both of my parents came to accept it as God's work, but in a positive way. They made every effort to love me as they loved my older brother, Kirk.

It appeared to others that I seemed to adjust to my situation fairly easily as a baby and toddler. Most children do in similar circumstances. Babies are instinctively adaptive and resilient. As I grew older, however, it was not unusual to be called "Captain Hook" or "Stubby" or some other creative name like "Ortho" and "Spaz" or just teased, laughed at, and even pushed around a bit. Those occurrences certainly were difficult and even painful. Many times I remember seeing other kids or teenagers walking towards me and I would cross the street so I was less likely to hear their remarks or get pushed around. I wasn't afraid of other kids, just not in a hurry to have my day ruined by hurt feelings. My parents never witnessed these instances or sensed that I was often hurting while dealing with being different. Outwardly I rarely displayed signs that it bothered me. To them I was a well-adjusted boy with no more or less difficulties growing up than Kirk or anyone else.

But I also learned at a pretty young age that I had a choice to make (life is all about choices); I could either sit in the corner of my room feeling sorry for myself for only having one hand or I could just go out and do whatever I really wanted to do. Even at that young age I chose wisely. I merely went out and did all those things that other kids did, especially boys, because I wanted to and believed I could.

One of the reasons that I made the decision to do whatever I wanted to, was that my parents and other close relatives didn't treat me any differently than they did my older brother, Kirk, and later my younger brother, Brian and much later our only sister, Valerie. Kirk was only fifteen months older than me, so in our early childhood we were very close playmates. I didn't feel different around him. Another influencing factor was that Dad taught us early on to believe that there was no such word as "can't." And he was living proof of that himself.

My father, William Robert "Bill" Effinger, was born on August 4, 1930 in Duluth, Minnesota. He was the first of two children to be born to Francis and Myrtle Effinger. Back then a radio was a luxury and food was cooled either in cellars beneath the homes and apartments or in an ice box that contained a 25 or 50-pound cake of ice delivered once a week by the "Iceman." Telephones were rare and usually hand-cranked to make them work. Phone numbers were prefixed with a name such as "Melrose" or "Richmond" followed by three digits.

Dad remembers playing in vacant fields with his friends until dinner time. In the warmer months there was plenty of fishing, running, biking, hiking and swimming. There was no television and certainly no video games to dull the senses of young, adventurous, and restless boys. In the winter Duluth saw no shortage of snow and ice allowing for abundant outdoor activities such as toboggan sliding, ice skating, sledding, skiing, and snowball fights. All in all life was pretty good at that time, despite the terrible depression. It was more harsh than today, certainly, but on average it was better than tolerable, for a while; World War II came with its own new problems and hardships. For the young Francis Effinger family, the war wasn't the worst event on the horizon.

In 1943 when Dad was only thirteen years old, my grandfather a neophyte hunter, agreed to go hunting with Leo, a relative who was experienced. This was in the middle of the Second World War. My grandfather didn't go deer hunting for the sport of it. He and the others went out of necessity to find food for the table; this was not unusual during the war and definitely not unusual given the circumstances; definitely common in the mid-west. It was only the second time in his life that my grandfather went hunting. It would be his last.

While standing near some trees, another hunter mistook the rustling of nearby branches to be a deer and pulled the trigger on his rifle. It was no deer. It was my grandfather. He didn't know what hit him. He died instantly.

Unfortunately, Dad had begun only recently before the deadly hunting accident to really get to know his father. Because he worked in the Roundhouse as a Boilermaker's Helper for the Northern Pacific Railroad and cut wood on the weekends with one of his brothers, my grandfather didn't have much free time to spend with his boys as he would have liked. The loss to the family was, of course, devastating, worsened later when two of grandfather's siblings also died that year - one from tuberculosis and one from a major heart attack.

With his father laid to rest, Dad became the man of the house, at least in his eyes. He worked at several jobs while going to school and early on developed a very strong work ethic. He washed windows; worked as stock-boy, set pins at the local bowling alley, shoveled snow, and did any other odd job he could find to earn money. He also decided that he would live his life to the fullest, to literally try to live for two, since his father's life had been so tragically cut short before his prime.

Not long after grandfather passed away, my grandmother, Dad, and his brother Jim moved to California where relatives had recently settled. Grandfather had often thought about relocating to California because he truly believed it was the land of opportunity.

My mother, Shirley Rae Bidwell, was born on January 25, 1929 in Mason City, Iowa at her grandparent's house. She lived with her parents in Mason City for seven years. A child of the Great Depression, my mother remembers wearing shoes with pieces of cardboard being cut and placed in the bare soles to extend their usefulness. Her mother made clothes for her out of hand-me-downs, including men's overcoats. At times food was so scarce that they lived on rice and soups of various kinds.

When Mom was seven years old she and her parents began moving around the country so that my grandfather could find work to support his family. A painter by trade, Robert Bidwell also played the banjo and ukulele whenever he had a little spare time. But most of the time he was working. Mom's favorite pastimes as a child and early teenager were drawing and coloring pictures, reading, roller skating and occasionally going to the movies… for a dime! She babysat when she was a teenager earning the un-Donald Trump-like sum of 25 cents a night, not per hour. Later she worked at her first real job as a department store clerk selling baby clothing.

During World War II my grandfather found work in California at the shipyards and the family settled in Hawthorne, a small suburb of Los Angeles where Mom ended up going to Luezinger High School. Money became a little easier to come by for them during the war, albeit through my grandfather's hard work. My mother's only sibling, Doyle, was born in October of 1944. My grandmother told me more than once that getting pregnant so many years after giving birth to my mother was a bit of a shock. For my mother, it also created some uncomfortable moments when she would take her baby brother out for a walk in his stroller; people thought the baby was hers and at 15 you can imagine the raised eyebrows she received, especially in the 1940s.

During her last semester in high school in 1947, Mom met my future father in art class. They were both creative and artistic. My father was an extrovert, to put it mildly, a bit of a charmer and had a great sense of humor. Mom was a tall, attractive, kind and generous young woman. Although Mom was a little over a year older that Dad they began dating and seeing each other quite often.

Following a great summer in sunny California, Dad's mother decided she wanted to move to Detroit, Michigan to be closer to more relatives. She hadn't enjoyed California as much as Dad did. My dad was not thrilled, but went to Detroit anyway. He enrolled at Cooley High School. On the first day of school he was told he couldn't take any of the classes he wanted so he decided to quit school and return to California and to his girlfriend. His mother was not happy about his decision, and believed he would not succeed in life by being so impetuous. She nonetheless became resigned to the idea. With $150 in his pocket he returned to the Golden State. He rented a room in

Inglewood, an adjacent town next to where my mother lived and began to look for work. Despite not having a father to turn to for advice and counsel, Dad believed he *could* and *would* achieve success in his life. He would do it for himself, but also for his father.

Dad took a job as an usher at a local movie theater on the day he arrived in California. Soon thereafter he was hired by Sears as a stock-boy where he worked until joining the United States Navy a few months later. While in the Navy he proposed to my mother. They were married on October 23, 1948.

My brother, Kirk, was born on August 16, 1949 in San Diego, California where Dad was stationed. While on a Naval training mission in Hawaii, unbeknown to my father, his six-week-old baby had come down with whooping cough and through some blunders at the naval hospital, had nearly died. When my father returned home he saw that Kirk was terribly dehydrated to the point where his skin could be lifted like paper and there was just bone underneath. Mom had been staying with her mother and the two of them also became quite ill.

After making his feelings known to his superiors in the Navy about what had happened, my father was given an honorable discharge to tend to his young ailing family. He had a very good record in the service, had been a good member of the team and promoted twice, but he had no plans to remain in the Navy and was happy to move on.

In 1950 my father became an apprentice carpenter and began what has become a more than sixty-year career in the construction and real estate industries. He took classes and worked hard to become a journeyman and later became job foreman. He soon discovered that by doing "piece work" or being paid based on how much work you produced in a day he could earn a lot more than union scale. Always the upwardly mobile guy that he was and still is at the age of 80, he got into piece work and prospered, despite others' admonishment that "you can't buck the unions." As Dad became more experienced and set examples of hard work and a willingness to do what it took to succeed he was becoming a leader.

My mother, father, me and Kirk (I'm on Mom's lap)

Growing Up "Different"

I was born on November 5, 1950 at Centinela Hospital in Inglewood, California. In most every way I was a healthy baby boy at nine-pounds and four-ounces, except, of course, for the obvious. The fingers on my right hand are a bit shorter than normal with the exception of my right thumb. I have a small thumb facing towards my body near the end of my left arm and two very small bumps on the opposite side that were the early beginnings of fingers that never fully developed. My feet are smaller than they otherwise should be and my toes are small. The tips of my big toes do not extend as far as other people's do. Other than these birth defects, thankfully, I'm "all here."

As I was growing up I asked my parents a couple of times why I had been born this way. The answer that stuck with me was, "We don't know for sure, Lynn, but God must have wanted you to be special." I didn't feel very special, at least not yet.

My early years from the time I was aware of my existence and surroundings were much like anyone else who grew up in the 1950s. For the first five years of my life we were a middle-class family of four living in a modest 900 square-foot, two-bedroom, one-bath house in Torrance, California. It was a cozy little home in a fairly new neighborhood, and only a few blocks from my mother's parent's house. That was great because my brother and I *loved* going to their home.

When our parents needed a babysitter my grandparents usually volunteered. "Doyle-Gramma" was the name we gave our grandmother because we associated her with our Uncle Doyle. She would make pancakes in the morning and Grampa would make hamburgers in the evening.

My grandfather played checkers with us and deftly played his banjo for us once in a while. I can still hear the uplifting twang emanating from his five-stringed traditional American instrument. Our times visiting them were great memories for us. We bugged Doyle quite a bit. We thought he was "cool," as he was several years older than us, but not an old uncle by any stretch. We liked being his shadow. I think at the time he wished he was invisible. He became even cooler in the late 1950s when he combed his blonde hair back in the ducktail style inspired by Elvis, Ed "Cookie" Burns and other popular figures with teenagers of the period.

We didn't get our first television set until Dad's mother, "Jimmy-Gramma" (same scenario), gave our family her old nine-inch black-and-white TV in 1954. I loved watching westerns, especially Hopalong Cassidy, The Lone Ranger, Roy Rogers, Gene Autry and all those goofy Republic Pictures western movies from the 1930s starring Marion Michael Morrison, aka, John Wayne. I also loved George Reeves as *Superman*, cartoons such as *Popeye, Bugs Bunny, Daffy Duck, Tom and Jerry* and so many others. Many of these classic cartoons were showed on television programs that had hosts in the greater Los Angeles market like Tom Hatton, dressed in a white sailor outfit and who played Popeye cartoons. We also had "Engineer Bill" with his "Happy Highball Engineers!" salute at the close of his program and his "red-light/green-light" game that got kids to drink a full glass of milk during his show. There was also "Skipper Frank" showing *Bugs Bunny* cartoons and later, Bozo the Clown.

Four of the best TV shows of the '50s and '60s as far as my brother and I were concerned were *Superman, The Adventures of Ozzie and Harriet,* the *Mickey Mouse Club* and the always entertaining, *Ed Sullivan Show*. Actually, we liked watching *Howdy Doody* better than the *Mickey Mouse Club*. Our parents thought it was far less educational than the *Mickey Mouse Club*, which was on at the same time of day. I learned to appreciate the *Mickey Mouse Club* much more as everybody's favorite Mousekateer, Annette, grew up and looked better and better in those sweaters (so much for educational programming). In 1956 Dad brought home our first family TV. It had a bigger, wider screen; still black and white, but much bigger than the nine-inch set Jimmy-Gramma had given to us a couple of years earlier.

The *Adventures of Ozzie and Harriet* was a terrific, funny show. It was interesting to be growing up and watching each season as David and Ricky Nelson were growing up as well, right before our eyes. David reminded me of Kirk; Reserved, studious, neat and tidy, and the oldest son. I was more like Ricky, at least to me. He was "irrepressible" which I wasn't really, but I certainly wasn't reserved, studious or neat and tidy, either. And I was the second son, a wise-cracker sometimes. Not in a disrespectful way, however. And, like Ricky, I found ways to get myself in a pickle more than once. Ozzie was nothing like Dad, but Mom shared qualities with Harriet; she was tall and beautiful, smart, talented, kind and understanding, and completely devoted to her husband and children.

As for *Superman*, what boy who ever read *Superman* comic books, watched the *Superman* serials at the movies or saw George Reeves play *Superman* on TV did not fantasize about having super powers to punish bad guys? In my particular case, I thought if I had been born on Krypton and came to earth, even if I only had one hand, nobody would mess with me. After all, I would be faster than a speeding bullet, more powerful than a locomotive, and able to leap tall buildings in a single bound! Tease me? Laugh at me? Push me around? I don't think so. You can imagine my chagrin when I saw the headline on the front page of the newspaper on June 17, 1959 that said, "Superman Dead" and the article chronicled the investigation into the death of George Reeves. The article speculated that he committed suicide (so much for super powers). Yeah, I knew he was just "playing" *Superman*, but suicide?

I was also enamored with TV shows and movies that depicted war stories and historical accounts of the bravery, patriotism and sacrifice of sailors, soldiers, pilots and others during World War II and the Korean War. Perhaps this was because Dad had served in the Navy, or simply because there were so many of them so soon after the war. I couldn't wait to grow up and serve in the military, preferably as a Marine. Day-dreamer that I was I could see myself valiantly protecting my family from the "enemy."

I also became a big fan of the underdog in its many forms: the *Ugly Duckling* (I cried like a baby the first time I saw Disney's version on TV because I related, intimately); the sports team up against a heavily favored opponent; a race horse that supposedly had no chance of winning; Jack-in-the-Box up against the mighty McDonald's; the gawky unattractive girl who was now competing for beauty queen, etc., etc., ad infinitum. It takes one to know one.

Growing Up "Different"

My mother used to walk me to kindergarten each morning and walked me home in the early afternoon. One beautiful fall morning we arrived at school and one of the girls in my class ran up to me and said that one of the other boys, a notorious bully, was picking on another girl. She asked me to help her get him to stop. The girls in my kindergarten class liked me. They were like the sisters I didn't have then and even motherly in a childlike way; they were protective of *me*.

Always wanting to see myself as a Knight in Shining Armor I went to the aid of the damsel in distress. Only the bully just pushed me away... twice. I kind of gave up. In an instant the kid turned on me. He pushed me to the ground, hitting me while I was lying on my back, prone to the world. I remember vividly looking up at the mothers who were there, including mine as I clutched my sack lunch that contained a delicate banana. The mothers were yelling at me to fight back. I only thought about not damaging my banana, which was in the brown paper bag I held tightly with my right hand. I was unable or unwilling to really mount much of a meaningful counterattack. Mom finally pulled the bully off me. I wasn't physically hurt, but emotionally I felt like a wimp. I decided that perhaps I needed to be a little tougher in such situations. It would be a while before I needed to be. I never again allowed myself to be that vulnerable. And I stopped taking bananas to school.

Another memorable and formative experience occurred following one of Dad's team-bowling nights when I was five years old. After his team won their match Dad saw an older gentleman on another lane who had an arm very similar to mine. Curious, he went up to the stranger and asked, "Excuse me sir, but do you tie your own shoes?" The man looked up at Dad as if he had two heads and replied, "Of course I do. They're tied aren't they?"

Dad apologized and explained to the man that he had a five-year-old son at home with one hand who didn't yet know how to tie his shoes. He was wondering if the man would show him how he tied his shoes so Dad could teach me. He showed Dad his method of tying his shoes, which he deftly did with the fingers and thumb on his one hand. Dad practiced and practiced until he too could tie his shoes dexterously one-handed.

With a noticeable air of excitement, Dad woke me up the next morning and showed me how he could tie his shoes with one hand and asked me to try it. I was impressed by his new talent. I did want to learn how to tie my shoes like Kirk could by age four, but not that much. In all honesty, I wasn't really in any hurry. If my shoe or shoes needed to be tied my mother had tied them. Sometimes Dad tied them. Sometimes Kirk even tied them or my grandparents would. Even my kindergarten teacher tied them. I didn't "need" to learn how to tie them. Because I wanted to obey my Dad's wishes, however, I watched him tie his shoes a few more times, trying to mimic his actions as he went along. It wasn't working for me. After several tries it still wasn't working and Dad sighed. He finally said that I should keep trying until I got the hang of it. But I didn't get the hang of it.

I didn't learn how to tie my own shoes until I was 11 years old. I'll explain the circumstances and the motivation for finally teaching myself to tie my shoes a little bit later, but suffice it to say here that in order to accomplish anything you have to have the desire to do so. You must possess the determination to overcome challenges; even small ones.

My first day in the first grade was also memorable. I had been enrolled at St. Catherine's Catholic School. When my mother brought me to school that first day we both realized something was amiss. As I entered the classroom to which I had been assigned Mom and I noticed that all the students were girls. Because my first name was "Lynn" the school administrator assumed I was female. Later in life being assigned to an all-girl class would have held some promise perhaps, but in first grade, not so much (I still receive mail addressed to "Ms. Lynn Effinger," which really only bothers me if the sender has met me. After all, what kind of impression could I possibly have made?).

I was quickly reassigned to an all-boy classroom and Mom started to leave. I was suddenly struck with panic at the realization that this wasn't kindergarten. Kindergarten was only half-days and I didn't know any of the kids in my class. This meant I'd no doubt have to endure teasing and bullying again. I began to cry. I wanted my mommy! I don't think I had ever cried for so long and so hard up until that point. A very kind priest came up to me and consoled me. He seemed so genuinely interested in me and making sure I was okay that I stopped crying and went to class. Things were alright after that for the most part, but boy, those nuns were tough, demanding and seemingly mean! I became much less concerned about the teasing and so forth from kids and did what I could to avoid the wrath of Sister Leticia. After all, I only had one set of knuckles.

My tenure at St. Catherine's was cut short. Our family was about to move to another home in another city. A new school and another round of "issues" were surely awaiting me I thought, but I was excited to move. We all looked forward to living in Orange County. I didn't yet realize how eventful the next few years would be.

Chapter Two

Baseball Fever

"No one can make you feel inferior without your consent."
— Eleanor Roosevelt

IN THE SUMMER OF 1956 our family moved to Buena Park, a relatively small but growing Southern California town. Buena Park at that juncture had once been bursting with orange groves and was most well known for being the home of Knott's Berry Farm. Back then Knott's Berry Farm was mostly that, a berry farm where one of Walter Knott's employees, Rudolph Boysen, invented the Boysenberry. Boysenberry syrup remains my absolute favorite pancake and waffle syrup to this day. Knott's was also an amusement park with a full-size steam-powered locomotive, stagecoaches, a replica of the Calico Gold Mine in the Mojave Desert in California, a merry-go-round, various shops, Mrs. Knott's famous fried chicken restaurant and more. Our new house was so close to Knott's that we heard the train whistle and the trained seals barking each evening.

One day during recess when I was in first grade at my new elementary school some older kids were teasing me and saying various things about my being a "cripple" and worse. After a while I felt I had heard enough. Without really saying much to defend my honor, I just decided to walk away. I came to the conclusion that I didn't want to go to school that morning and continued walking, right out of the playground and outside the school fence. I kept walking until I got to Knott's Berry Farm. You could walk most everywhere at Knott's back then. There was no admission fee to the general park area. You simply bought a ticket to go on individual rides or see certain exhibits. I walked around for quite a while and then decided to climb onto one of the ponies on the Merry-Go-Round. The attendant strapped me in and then asked me for my ticket. Then he said, "Oh, I must have already gotten it from you." I didn't know if he meant what he said or was just giving me a free ride. It didn't matter much to me either way. I was riding the Merry-Go-Round!

When the Merry-Go-Round stopped revolving, the attendant helped me down from the pony and I climbed off. I decided I should walk toward home, even though I was probably going to be in trouble for leaving school unattended. I was not yet 6 years old. I didn't realize in just how much trouble I would be. As I was waiting to cross Beach Boulevard at the stoplight when it would turn green, a police car came by and pulled up next to me. A young police office got out of the car and walked up to me. He then asked me where I was going. I told him what had happened at school and that I was walking home. I conveniently left out the part about walking around at Knott's and riding the Merry-Go-Round. He asked me where I lived and then asked me to get into the police car. They took me home.

Gee, was Mom ever happy to see me get out of that police car... *not!* She was very upset with me and scolded me. The fact that I told her about the other kids and their comments lessened the duration, but because she was worried that I might do this again was still mad at me. She said she wasn't going to tell Dad, which made me feel a little better. But when Dad arrived home that evening she went ahead and told him about it. I thought I was in trouble big time now. But, after explaining the whole situation to him, he was not upset with me. He did however explain that I had done wrong and he made me quite aware that I had put myself in potential danger and that I must never do such a thing again. He told me to go right to my teacher and tell her if kids ever said those things to me again, but never to leave school by myself.

On October 12, 1956 my younger brother, Brian became the newest member of the Effinger family. Another boy was added to the mix. Over the years Brian became quite entertaining in many ways and we came to learn that he was so intelligent that you might say he was "from another world." He was also the most musically-inclined among us, years later learning to play the organ. The age difference between Brian, and Kirk and me made it difficult for the three of us to be as close as Kirk and I had been. This caused some "interesting" situations over the years, but Brian is a great person. He survived all that and more and became a wonderful husband, father and now grandfather, sharing many great years together with his wife, Minda and their beautiful family.

Dad was working hard on construction sites at this time as a framing contractor. Some of his new friends in the community saw in his drive, energy, enthusiasm, political interests and leadership skills a person who might be an asset to the growth and economic development of Buena Park. They encouraged him to get involved in the Junior Chamber of Commerce, which he did. Shortly thereafter Dad was elected President of the Jaycees, as they were commonly known. And my mother soon after that was elected President of the Jaycee-ettes, the female version of the pro-business organization. They were both respected and displayed noticeable leadership qualities.

Dad did such an impressive job that he was approached to run for the City Council of Buena Park. At the age of 28 my dad was elected to the City Council and in very short order became the city's Mayor. He was one of the youngest mayors in America at that time. He just wouldn't listen when people, especially the "established" few said, "You can't get elected here, boy," and proved them wrong.

I did my part one day to help Dad get elected. I had overheard a conversation he had with Mom and my grandmother, Myrtle. They were talking about needing to raise money for Dad's campaign. So I found a tin can and went around the neighborhood collecting change from our neighbors. When I got home later that afternoon with my tin can nearly filled with change, I presented it to Dad. He was mortified! He told me to go right back to every house where I had received money and give it back. I was a little hurt at first. But he explained that it wasn't a good thing for me to go around trying to collect money from our neighbors. He was perfectly capable of raising the money he needed for his campaign. I told him I couldn't go back. I didn't know who had given me what amount of change! Dad just smiled and said, "Okay, we'll keep the money. But please don't do that again." He was still smiling, so I figured what I had done was not that bad. It was my first attempt at "fundraising."

Dad was developing into a genuine community leader who commanded attention just by entering a room.

This was a quality I recognized early on whenever I had the opportunity to see him interact with other adults.

———

In the late-1950s I became captivated with baseball. I loved everything about it. I read a book about Babe Ruth and couldn't find out enough about him and other baseball greats. I saw the movie about Babe Ruth starring William Bendix on TV and thought how wonderful it must have been to be the "Great Bambino." When the Brooklyn Dodgers moved to Los Angeles I thought that was incredible good fortune. Brooklyn's great loss was Southern California's tremendous gain. I had only seen baseball up close when I watched Dad play softball for the Junior Chamber of Commerce. Once in a while there were big league games on TV and during the World Series our teachers would sometimes let us listen to the games on battery-powered transistor radios at school.

Whenever possible I watched baseball games on television. "Wow, baseball is awesome!" I thought. "I'd sure like to play baseball like Willie Mays, Duke Snyder, Mickey Mantle, Ernie Banks, Warren Spahn, Hank Aaron and other big league heroes when I grow up!" It honestly never occurred to me that although I didn't have a left hand I wouldn't be able to play baseball. Why on earth not, I wondered?

Seeing that I loved baseball so much, Dad bought me my first baseball glove in 1958. It was a dark brown Spalding mitt. Although kind of flat like a pancake, I loved it! I loved the smell of the leather! I loved the feel of it! I tossed a baseball into the webbing cradled in my left arm over and over and over again to "break it in." I even slept with it. Who needed a teddy bear at the age of eight? I'm going to play baseball! I had baseball fever.

Dad taught me how to catch and throw the baseball. He and I played catch once in a while, when he wasn't working of course, which was most of the time since he had a regular day-job and served as Mayor of Buena Park. But we did play catch in the front yard from time to time. He taught me to cradle my glove in the bend of my left elbow, throw the ball with my right hand and then maneuver the glove onto my hand... quickly. It sounds clunky I know, but when you practice it over and over and over again it becomes much less so. It became a smooth process in no time at all and I just felt natural doing it. I slipped the mitt on and off like a warm knife through butter. Well, maybe not that smoothly.

Alan Kinnard, a classmate of mine also played catch with me. He was available more often than Dad. Sometimes I would just go in the back yard and pitch the baseball against the fence. Not good for our wooden grape-stake fence, but I was going to practice one way or another. Later my parents bought me a "Dodger Pitch-Back." The Pitch-Back was a metal framed contraption about three feet square that had an elastic net attached to it so that when you threw a baseball against it the ball would bounce back so you could catch your own pitch; Pretty cool.

In the 1950s, boys (only boys) could play Little League Baseball starting at the age of eight. I told my parents and all my friends that I wanted to play Little League Baseball. They had real uniforms! My parents were enthusiastic supporters of this goal; some of my friends, not so much. Most of them said no one would let me play Little League Baseball. I asked why not? They said, "Because, who wants a one-armed kid on their team? Coaches want guys who can really play, and you can't." Well, I returned fire saying in essence, "yes I can, yes I will, just watch me."

When playing catch or playing baseball at school I was pretty good or at least I thought I was. I was determined to play Little League Baseball just like most all of my friends. Well, the day had finally arrived for Little League tryouts in the spring. Dozens and dozens of young boys were there early in the morning at the dusty baseball fields with their fathers hoping to do well enough to make a team. And so was I. I had been practicing, but at eight years old I really wasn't too hot of a prospect after all, especially with the bat. I didn't make contact with one pitch during tryouts. I also flubbed a couple of the grounders hit my way and dropped a pop fly.

At school the following week most all of my classmates who had also tried out had been contacted by team managers to become a member of their teams. Not me, and I wondered why not, despite my poor performance at tryouts. Unknown to me at the time, Dad went to one of the managers and told him how much I loved baseball and how good it would be for me to be on a team. Back then there was no guarantee that a kid would be on a team and get to play, ever, let alone play in each game. I don't know if it was the fact that the manager had a soft spot in his heart for this eight-year-old little boy with one hand or the fact that Dad was mayor or what, but I soon became a proud member of the Braves. I was thrilled... but only temporarily.

On the night of the first practice I was dropped off by my mother and instructed to go tell the manager that I was there and ready to practice. I was still very shy around strangers, especially adults and I didn't see any other kids on the team who I knew. I was so shy I just walked over to the backstop and stood there, like a fence post, not saying anything to anyone and no one made any effort to speak to me either. I watched the whole practice from behind the wire backstop. When Mom picked me up she asked me how practice had gone. I told her my sad story and she relayed that to Dad that night.

My father got that straightened out and at the next practice the manager, his assistant coach and the team welcomed me to the Braves. I went to all the practices, often early. Mom drove me to every one of them. I always tried my best in practice. It took me a while to stop turning my head to the right when a fly ball came screaming out of the sky, falling toward my nose, but I got better and better over time. I enjoyed being with my teammates at practice. I loved going to the games in my Braves uniform; gray flannel pants and shirt with green striping and lettering, green stirrup socks with white stripes, and a green baseball cap. I often arrived before the other players because I was so excited to be on the team and expected to actually get to play in a game soon.

I learned the hard way that there was no guarantee of playing often… or ever. A perennial bench warmer, I felt more like the team mascot than a true teammate. I couldn't have gotten more splinters in my rear if I'd sat on a split-rail fence. All the guys were nice to me, but they rarely treated me as an equal. No wonder. I was on that team for two years but I didn't get to play in a real game until the last inning of the last game of the *second* year. I walked my only time at bat and stood out in right field until the game was over. Not a very auspicious start to my athletic "career."

I was fairly coordinated, although I was not a natural athlete. No one in my family had ever really distinguished themselves in sports, so it was no real surprise that I had to work hard to be any good. I was good within the school environment. But Little League was a step up and only the better young athletes played with regularity. My early experience with Little League disappointed me to be sure, but I didn't give up on wanting to play. Not just be on a team, but actually play in games. One of the traits I am most grateful for inheriting from my father is tenacity. In order to persevere, one must have the desire to succeed, work hard and be tenacious. I have, because I did and I am. And because I would not let others make me feel inferior, Little League Baseball was about to get a whole lot more fun!

We moved to Long Beach, California in 1960. By this time Dad was working for S&S Construction Company, a growing new home development company located in Beverly Hills, California founded by Nathan and David Shapell and their brother-in-law, Max Webb. Nathan and David hired Dad to be their land man while he was still serving as Mayor of Buena Park. It was his responsibility to search out opportunities to purchase tracts of land suitable enough and potentially profitable enough to build new home developments in the greater Los Angeles and Orange County areas. We moved into an S&S home in Long Beach just across Seventh Street from what was then Long Beach State College because that shortened Dad's commute by over an hour.

My parents liked the climate of this coastal community and all that it had to offer, including a large marina where Dad kept our 32-foot converted cabin cruiser (it had been an old wooden fishing boat but since Dad was a skilled carpenter he was able to build onto it a beautifully appointed cabin). We all grew to like Long Beach. There were a lot of great places to go and many divergent things to do. On Sundays after church in the early years that we lived there our family would have breakfast at Hody's, a popular restaurant in the Park Estates section of town. The food was great, but one of the things I remember most about the place was the clear plastic partitions separating the booths. Embedded in them were butterflies of many different types. Real butterflies! The other thing I remember was the balloons the waitresses gave to kids that looked like Hody the Clown when blown up. They had cardboard feet that you attached at the bottom that made the balloons stand up on their own. Brian got one each week. Ah, memories of simple pleasures!

———

As I mentioned earlier, Dad was raised in a devout Catholic family. He had even been an altar boy at St. Elizabeth's Church in Duluth and his family attended mass each Sunday. He had attended a Catholic School in his early years. I was subsequently raised in a Catholic home, as well. Church was a very important part of our lives. Although I wasn't thrilled to have to dress up each Sunday morning to attend mass, I became a true believer. I came to enjoy mass because of its solemn formality, the beauty of the church with colorful stained-glass windows, the melodic sound of Latin and the messages of the Gospel. I became convinced that prayer was powerful. That Jesus is the savior of mankind and that I truly had a "Guardian Angel" looking out for me. I believed in prayer so much in fact that I more than once fell asleep after praying that I would wake up to discover that I now had a left hand. Alas, I eventually discovered that prayers are powerful, but not *that* powerful.

Construction on Kettering Elementary School where Kirk and I were supposed to attend in Long Beach wasn't yet completed at the beginning of the school year in September of 1960. All of us kids who lived in our new home community were bussed across town to Buffum Elementary School. At first I didn't seem to run into too much hazing or harassment from the kids while at Buffum, but one day not long after the school year commenced that changed.

Our teacher had the boys play softball one afternoon. Now, no one had baseball gloves at school, so you did the best one could be expected to by cupping your two hands together without a mitt to catch the ball when you were in the field. I was playing center field when one of the opposing team's batters hit a high bouncing ball out past the shortstop towards me. There were runners at first and second base so it was important that I catch the ball and toss it to the catcher at home plate to prevent a run or runs from scoring. We were ahead 2-0 at that point.

I had been on a Little League team for two years and had progressed to be a better baseball player (at least in practice), so I didn't think anything of simply catching the bouncing ball and making the throw. Only I didn't catch the ball. I stuck up my right hand with my shorter-than-normal fingers and tried to snatch the ball the same way I had hundreds of times, but this time without a big old mitt. The ball bounced off my hand and rolled for a week (or so it seemed) before I could chase it down, pick it up and throw it to the impatient, waiting infielders.

Three runs scored. I immediately heard guys yelling at me, "Ortho!" and "What a Spaz!" and worse. Here I was playing the one sport that I knew I was pretty good at, even better than some of these guys, but I made a huge error and they let me have it. There was no joy in Mudville. The game ended with us losing of course and so too ended my respite from negative comments, dirty looks and teasing. My feelings and my pride were equally hurt. Welcome to Long Beach, Lynn.

Over time things got better, especially when baseball tryouts came in April. By then we had moved into our new school and I was getting to know my classmates and neighborhood kids better. They were getting to know me better as well. We had played pick-up two-hand touch football games in the fall and winter and although I was usually picked last by the team captain, or rather I was the last guy not yet picked; I had distinguished myself as a competent center, blocker and "tackler." We didn't actually tackle anyone. As a ball carrier you were down or "tackled" if you were touched by a defensive player. Here I actually had an advantage over the other players. In touch football the players agreed that you had to touch the ball carrier with two hands for them to be officially "down." But they decided, thankfully, that the ball carrier would be officially down if I touched him with one hand. I know, generous of them, right? But they could have just as easily said I couldn't play football with them at all. I actually made every effort to touch the ball carrier with my hand and my arm, but wasn't always successful in that regard.

I had distinguished myself enough to at least earn the opportunity to play. The older kids tended to respect me more than the kids who were my own age, for whatever reason. One of my classmates that I admired most for his athletic ability and because he seemed to genuinely like and respect me was Wes Edwards. Wes was well-liked and a great guy to hang out with. He was a good football player and baseball player and also a southpaw, so he fielded the baseball with his mitt on his right hand, just like me. This meant I could watch him and mimic him to learn to how be a better fielder. I learned a lot from Wes over the years and I still value his friendship tremendously.

As Little League tryouts approached in the spring of 1961 I was able to again play catch with Dad when he had time, which wasn't very often. Sometimes I played catch with Kirk or more often with Wes and other kids in the neighborhood or at school after class and on weekends.

33

These classmates could now see that perhaps I wasn't an "Ortho" after all. My abilities playing touch football, my sense of humor and empathy and kindness towards my female classmates earned me an escape from teasing and entrance into the clique of the "accepted ones," if not the popular ones.

By this time Mom had given me a little crystal radio that looked like a wristwatch. I could pick up a Rock 'N Roll station or two, but the most important station was KMPC... the "Dodgers Station!" I listened intently to Dodgers baseball games every night while throwing a baseball into the webbing of my Spalding glove.

"Hello everybody; It's time for Dodgers baseball." Oh, the sweet sound of Vin Scully's voice! He was so good he made Farmer John hot dog commercials sound like a soliloquy from Shakespeare. He made me feel like I was there at the game. The stats; the players' backgrounds, the excitement and cheers of the crowd and the action! Wow, I loved baseball more than anything at this point and couldn't wait to try out again!

On the day of tryouts for the Los Altos Little League at El Dorado Park in Long Beach, at the age of ten, I did much better than I had when we lived in Buena Park. I caught several ground balls and pop flies in the field. And although I didn't get a clean hit when it was my turn at bat, I did make good contact. My hand-eye coordination was coming around nicely.

Without "political" intervention this time, I was actually picked by "Lonnie" (sadly I don't remember his last name), the popular manager of the Pirates to be on his team. He admired my enthusiasm for the game and my abilities under the circumstances. Another reason he selected me may well have been that his oldest son had been involved in a terrible accident and his left arm, his pitching arm, had been severely burned by fire. He had to overcome much adversity and pain on his own to be able to play baseball at the high level he once did, and he had succeeded. I had earned the opportunity to be on a team through my performance at tryouts... and probably because of the empathy of Lonnie. Maybe I still wasn't a hot prospect, but I made a team, just like my friends who had also tried out.

Mom began shuttling me to and from practices again. I was a little bigger, a little stronger and more knowledgeable about the game of baseball. At ten years old I was in the middle range of players relative to my age. Kids on our team were ages eight through 12. In practice I began to make good contact with the ball when I was at the plate. I absolutely loved being at bat. In my mind's eye I saw myself as a typical right-handed batter. I held the bat above my right shoulder with my right hand and "held" or rather rested my left arm under my right hand against the bat. But to me I envisioned myself holding the Louisville Slugger with two hands. When I swung at a pitch I also felt that I was doing so just like any other hitter. Even though my left arm no longer touched the bat as I swung hard, to my "thinking" I was still helping to control the bat with my left arm. I'm sure to others it looked more like I was the caveman comic-strip character, *Alley Oop* swinging a club instead of a bat with one hand, but that's not how it seemed to me.

Me at the age of 10, bat in hand.

I didn't get to play in every game that year, but I played in most of them. I played right field most of the time, but I played. I made decent catches on fly balls and grounders and because my right arm was getting much stronger, my throws back to the infielders were harder and more accurate. And I was starting to hit the ball more frequently. As your physical skills improve your mental approach to the game improves as well. Actually *playing* baseball is a heck of a lot more fun than watching it or being the team mascot. We finished the season just a little over .500, but it was a very satisfying experience. I not only proved that I could play baseball, my friends were now much more impressed with my ability. Lonnie had taken an interest in helping me to become an improved baseball player and I was grateful for the respect and kindness he had shown to me all season long.

Baseball Fever

On November 27, 1961, an event took place that Dad had hoped for since my parents were first married. Following a wonderful Thanksgiving dinner while Kirk and I and our younger brother, Brian were comfortably basking in the fullness that accompanies turkey, dressing, mashed potatoes and gravy, peas, cranberry sauce, and yes, pumpkin pie, Mom was going into labor. Dad had wanted a baby girl for many years, but to no avail. So far, our family was comprised of Mom, Dad and three boys.

Without ultrasound machines or other reliable methods to determine the sex of an unborn baby, everyone in our extended family held their collective breath for months after Mom announced her pregnancy, all hoping that Dad's wish would come true. I was ambivalent about whether the baby would be a boy or a girl at first I guess. But when Dad came home from the hospital and woke us up to tell us that we now had a sister, Valerie Jean, I enthusiastically joined in the chorus of, "Yippee, way to go Mom!" The youngest of four children and the only girl had arrived; the sweet little girl my father had been waiting for all those years.

When I was in the sixth grade in 1962 I was well established in school, had many good friends and generally enjoyed living in Long Beach at that time very much. As spring approached it meant one important thing to me – baseball tryouts were near! A little taller, a little stronger and more experienced at baseball since getting to play quite a lot the previous year on the Pirates, I was really looking forward to this new season.

In early spring I came down with a bad case of mumps on both sides of my throat and at the same time developed stomach flu. I don't need to describe to you how awful that combination was. I was really sick and bed-ridden for over two weeks. To this day I can't even look at a box of Sugar Crisp cereal. In addition to the pain, the boredom was tough to take. The only thing I really enjoyed, which is kind of sad to admit today, was watching *Felix the Cat* cartoons. Felix and his "Bag of Tricks," the Professor, Rock Bottom, the Master Cylinder, and Va-Voom and I shared each afternoon together; Corny, but entertaining to a sick kid.

One afternoon toward the end of my illness Dad peeked into our bedroom that Kirk and I shared and threw me something. It was a brand new baseball glove! I went to work on it immediately to break it in by throwing the ball into the pocket and webbing while cradled in the bend of my left elbow. Tryouts weren't far off and I needed the mitt to be as ready as I was. It was even easier to put on and take off than my old one. It was one of the greatest gifts I had ever received up to that point and I thanked Dad profusely for having bought it for me. I quickly recovered shortly thereafter and returned to school and to practicing baseball with friends.

During tryouts in April I fielded every grounder and fly ball hit to me. At bat I hit the ball with some new-found authority, didn't miss a pitch and felt completely comfortable at the plate. I was chosen to play for the Phillies.

That baseball season was a turnaround season for me. I believe my mental attitude contributed to that as much as my improved physical ability. As one of several 11-year-old kids on the team I played first base and was one of our starting pitchers. I made many plays at first base and to the astonishment of more than one opposing team I could catch a ground ball, take off my glove, grab the ball and throw it in a smooth enough manner to turn a double play. As a pitcher I had my ups and downs, but I loved being on the mound. Pitching required me to put my mitt on after each pitch very quickly. A batter smacking the ball hard right back at me that I had just pitched to him would be an interesting occurrence to be sure. That year I never dropped a ball that was hit back at me while on the mound.

Although I played well at first base on a regular basis, I remember making one particularly noteworthy catch one afternoon against the team coached by Lonnie, my former manager of the Pirates the previous year. A kid hit the ball on a line drive over the first base line that looked to everyone to be hit well over my head. From where I was standing just to the right of first base I quickly spun around and jumped up just in time to backhand the screaming liner. Whap! Into my mitt it went. Lonnie had a great big smile on his face and praised me in front of all the players and their parents. I think he felt a little pride in believing, and rightly so, that he had helped to make me a better baseball player.

Despite all the praise I began receiving from my parents, relatives, friends and teachers for my fielding ability; it was my hitting that earned me the most satisfaction and recognition. As the number three batter in the lineup I was up to bat several times each game and I was now playing the full six innings of every Little League game that season. My skills had improved that much. I struck out a few times, naturally, as everyone does. But I started hitting the ball all over the field. I wasn't a true power hitter, but I made contact most every time I was at the plate. That year my batting average was over .400. Now, I realize today as I did then that this was in Little League, but that high of a batting average at any level of play is pretty darned good for a kid, especially a kid who only has one hand. Playing baseball that year was very gratifying, indeed.

As described earlier, Dad tried to encourage me to learn how to tie my shoes by myself when I was five. Regrettably, for Dad at least, I still had not mastered this very basic task as of the summer of 1962. Well, I was going to be in seventh grade come this September and entering junior high school. I was a pre-teen whose voice cracked from time to time. I began to have more interest in girls than ever before. And I knew I was going to be more than a little embarrassed if I couldn't tie my own shoes. Why did this news flash hit me that particular summer, the endless summer of The Beach Boys, Jan and Dean, the Annette Funicello and Franky Avalon *Beach-Blanket* movies, etc., etc.? In what class in junior high school do you have to tie your shoes… each and every day? You guessed it, gym class. No way was I going to ask a classmate, gym teacher or anyone else to please tie my shoes. No way. Can you just imagine the fallout I would have received from that kind of request? I sure could.

I learned many years later by reading his best-selling book, *Think and Grow Rich*, author Napoleon Hill believed that desire is the starting point of all achievement. It didn't matter that I had yet to read this brilliant tome on personal success in 1962; I had then developed a serious desire to teach myself how to tie my shoes. In fact, beyond desire, I had become driven. That would be required if I was going to learn this skill, basic as it might be.

One clear, sunny afternoon in August of 1962, just a few weeks before school would begin our family was down at the Long Beach Marina hanging out on our boat. My parents had just bought me a new pair of low-top tennis shoes for gym class, so I wore them that day. At some point I was alone sitting up on the front deck staring down at my bright, white, canvas and rubber sneakers. I don't remember how long I sat there staring, but I know it was quite a while. I reached down for the laces, which were longer than any shoe laces I had ever seen. I suspected they could have been used as a tow rope. Anyway, I started to recall the method of tying my shoes that Dad had learned from the gentleman at the bowling alley so many years before, attempting in vain to teach me. I recalled the process and tried it. I tried it more than once. It wasn't coming together, but I refused to give up. This particular method required you to use only the fingers and thumb on one hand to accomplish the desired result. Okay, I thought, if that's not going to work for me, what will?

About that time Dad yelled up to me that we were going up to the café to get some hamburgers for lunch. I yelled back to him that I didn't want to eat. I was learning to tie my shoes. Now, I couldn't see his face or that of my mother, but I could have sworn I heard somebody say, "I've heard that before." Undeterred, I went back to my task.

Staring once again at the long shoe laces of my left shoe, I decided to twist the two laces over one another, then wrap one of the laces around my little thumb at the end of my left arm and hold it tight through leverage applied. Then I pulled on the other lace with my right hand, which I did; so far, so good. Now I simply made a loop with lace number one, held it down with the top of my left arm, then wrapped lace number two around it and tried to push it through making the second loop. This delicate operation was a little trickier to coordinate, so I had to try more than once. Just as I was getting the second loop through successfully my parents and Kirk came down the gangplank in front of the boat. I got the lace through, pulled on it to lengthen the loop and held it down with the top of my left arm and pulled the second loop tight. As they got right up to the bow of the boat I rose quickly and started jumping up and down yelling, "I did it, I did it, I did it!" My parents literally had tears in their eyes. So too, did I.

I learned a valuable lesson that day. In order to accomplish something, especially something that is difficult or challenging, you must want deep down inside of you to accomplish it. You must have desire and tenacity to succeed. Even at age eleven that lesson stuck with me. I was about to apply it again during my last season of Little League Baseball. I couldn't wait for spring to put my desire and improved skills to work to accomplish my goal of making next season my very best ever.

Chapter Three

The Center-Fielder of Attention

"Do not let what you cannot do interfere with what you can do."

– John Wooden

The Center-Fielder of Attention

THE YEAR 1963 WOULD BE my last year to play Little League Baseball. The age limit was 12, an age I had reached the previous November. As with every year for five years, I was anxiously awaiting spring and baseball tryouts. I began practicing earlier in the year than ever. I was hoping to play Pony League the following year and knew that managers from that league would be scouting our Little League games looking for the most promising future prospects. I was going to be ready.

But first, in the year that saw a quarter of a million Americans participate in the civil rights March on Washington, D.C. where Reverend Martin Luther King, Jr. made his now famous "I have a dream" speech on the steps of the Lincoln Memorial, I had my own experience with discrimination. While in no way compared to the ugly bigotry and hatred foisted upon African Americans at that time, especially in the Deep South, my experience was terribly distressing to me, nonetheless. Everything is relative. This was personal.

One day just a few weeks after I entered Hill Junior High School I was called to the school nurse's office. I wasn't sick or anything and had no idea why I was asked to go see her. A nice lady greeted me at the nurse's office and asked me to have a seat. After doing as she requested somewhat reluctantly, she then asked me how I felt that day and made some other small talk before getting right to the heart of why I was in her office.

It turned out that Mr. Kelb, my physical education instructor, had gone to the nurse and told her that I should be transferred from his gym class to "Special Gym Class."

Students referred to Special Gym Class unfeelingly as "Ortho Gym." The kids who were relegated to that class had serious physical and/or mental disabilities. Most if not all of these kids truly benefited from such special attention and alternative activities, such as ping pong, playing checkers and other games. They were kids just like everyone else, but treated and looked upon differently from the "normal" students. That was and is most unfortunate and unfair. I was shocked and hurt to think that I would share their exiled fate. Not because I felt better or more important than these special kids, but because I had played many sports and performed at least as well as my classmates and others, especially when playing baseball. I told the nurse about playing first base and about pitching. And I stressed to her how well I could hit. After all, my batting average last year was over .400, I exclaimed!

"Why did he say that?" I asked her, trying to hold back the flood of tears that began to well up in my eyes. She told me that Mr. Kelb felt that because I had difficulty climbing the rope, doing pull-ups and performing a couple of other gymnastic exercise routines that all the other kids were doing, I should be placed in Special Gym for my own good. Now it was impossible to hold back the tears. Through watery eyes I pleaded with the nurse not to make me go to Special Gym Class. I said that gymnastics would end soon and we'd be playing sports at which I was much better. I also told her that I would be devastated if my friends and especially those who didn't know me well or didn't like me for whatever adolescent reasons they may have had found out I had been assigned to Special Gym. "And what will my parents think of me," I asked? Then she gently cradled

The Center-Fielder of Attention

my hand into both of hers and almost whispered, "Lynn, I know your mother well. I know how good you are at playing baseball and that you have handled being born without a left hand exceptionally well... and that your mom and dad are very proud of you and love you very much."

She said that she had no intention of transferring me out of Mr. Kelb's gym class despite his unfounded concerns. But before she made that decision she said she had wanted to hear how I felt about the situation to make sure that I believed that I should not be reassigned. The nurse then told me that I was an example of how perseverance overcomes adversity and that I must always strive to do my very best. Upon conclusion of this mostly uncomfortable meeting she wished me well and asked me to say hello to my mother. I composed myself immediately so that no one would see that I had been so upset and returned to class. A little shaken, but not broken.

I cannot tell you how relieved I was to know that this matter would not come up again. Nor how mad I was at Mr. Kelb, who I believed just didn't want to be bothered by someone of "my kind." When I got home I told Mom what had happened and she gave me a huge hug, engulfing me in pure motherhood and affection. She told me that the nurse had called her on the telephone and explained what had happened. There would be no transfer. I cried again, but these tears were more out of joy than sadness.

Once again, despite a potentially disastrous experience I rose above the situation and prepared for my finest hour playing Little League Baseball. With my Mr. Kelb experience behind me I could move on and get ready for Little League tryouts in the spring. Oh, sure, I had to concentrate on my school work as well, because without good grades there could be no baseball. That was always stressed at our home. Thankfully, in junior high I was focused on my studies and did pretty well. Einstein I wasn't, but I held my own. I was also a bit distracted by girls at this point, but since so few girls gave me a second thought unless they were looking for someone "safe" to talk to or confide in, it turned out to be less of an issue than perhaps I had wanted it to be.

Unfortunately, in junior high students begin to be more conscious of differences between students and start choosing whom among the unwashed the various members of cliques will accept into their sphere. While I tended to get along and fit in with kids of most interests and persuasions, the "in crowd" sometimes shunned me and even made fun of me. I admit that I was a little pudgy, awkward, wore glasses and wasn't as stylish a dresser as members of that supposedly elite group, not to mention my other obvious physical difference, but I was athletic and not Quasimodo. I was often miffed that I was being dissed. I found myself coming close to physically defending myself on a couple of occasions, but was able to avoid mixing it up because the instigators or tormentors often had a bigger bark than bite. I also didn't go out for any school athletic teams because I was content playing Little League Baseball. Not to worry, I thought, I knew to where and when I would escape.

Baseball tryouts were more fun this time than at any other period in my Little League "career." I fielded with the best of them. When I threw over to first base from the shortstop position my arm had gotten so much stronger that each throw was fast, but a little high. This would prove to be to my benefit later as I would discover. But once again my hitting ability separated me from most of the other kids that day. I hit every pitch, hard and into the deep outfield. Very pleased with my performance, Lonnie selected me to play for him once again.

Lonnie told me that because my right arm was so much stronger than anyone else on the team he wanted me to play center field. I thought that was cool, because my idols, Willie Mays, Mickey Mantle and Duke Snyder all played center field! And even better still, he wanted me to bat fourth in the batting order – "Cleanup," as that spot in the lineup is commonly called, which is generally reserved for a team's best hitter.

We practiced at Long Beach State College. At this point I loved practice as much as I did the actual games, especially when it was my turn to practice hitting. Lonnie's son was in high school and played on his school's varsity baseball team. He often came to our practices and was a constant inspiration to me and I appreciated all the advice he was willing to give me. He had become a star pitcher at his high school, which I believe was Millikan High. It impressed me no end that he had been through a tragic fire and overcame great adversity to achieve success. I knew I had it much easier than he did. After all, I was born without a left hand. I didn't know any other way to be. But he had been "normal" before the accident. He remembered what it was like not to have such terrible scar tissue all over his throwing arm that impeded his ability to pitch.

He was a positive role model for me and I will never forget his passion for playing baseball.

Playing center field was a great experience. Next to playing shortstop and pitching I think it's the best position on the team. You can clearly see everything that's going on. I had good range and could chase down fly balls in a wide area. Because of my strong arm I could throw the ball with velocity virtually anywhere on the field, and my accuracy had further improved, which meant that defensively I was on top of my game.

As the season progressed I kept close tabs on my batting average. Still more of a percentage hitter than a power slugger I had a hit and got on base virtually every other time I was at bat. I was recognized by my teammates as a leader on our team.

Game after game I kept hitting on a pace I had never expected but certainly dreamed of. And I started hitting the ball deeper with more consistency. It was a wonderful experience. Yes, I loved making the running catches and throwing out base runners, but batting in the cleanup position and contributing mightily to our team's success and winning record were paramount. Doing your best, achieving personal goals and being a part of a successful team in athletics prepares you for the competitive world beyond sports. It teaches you that while individuality is important, teamwork can help you accomplish so much more. It is as true in business and for families as it is in athletics, as I would later learn.

Although my batting average was just under .500 by the last game of the season, in five years I still had never hit a home run over the fence; the ultimate accomplishment for hitters. I was disappointed that I hadn't, but my average was so high and the runs I drove in were so many that I didn't dwell on it. Then, during the final game of that season on my first trip to the plate, something almost surreal occurred. When it was my turn to bat, I walked slowly from the on-deck circle toward home plate. The umpire, an older kid who had been our umpire a couple of times before, said hello. Then he said to me, "I've seen you hit quite a few singles and doubles, but I bet you can't hit a home run."

Whenever someone challenges me and doubts that I can accomplish something, I tend to get a little fired up inside. This time was no different. I turned to him and with a smirk on my face I simply said to him, "Yes I can, yes I will, just watch me."

The pitcher began his wind up, reached back and then let the ball fly towards home plate and the catcher's waiting glove. I swung too hard and fouled it off. He wound up again. As the next pitch left the pitcher's hand things seemed to go in slow motion. I saw the ball clearly, getting closer and closer. I could almost read "Rawlings" on the face of the ball. I swung smoothly but with enough velocity to make contact cleanly and sent the ball soaring high out into left-center field. I dropped the bat and started heading for first base, my eyes riveted on the ball's trajectory. The ball seemed frozen in mid-air. Suddenly, as I rounded first base the ball flew over the center fielder's outstretched glove and fell beyond the left-center field fence! Remarkably, as God is my witness, I had hit my first Little League home run. I was jumping up and down as I rounded the remaining bases, my feet seemingly not touching the ground until I reached home plate where Lonnie was waiting for me with open arms. I stomped on home plate and just smiled at the umpire who couldn't believe I had done it either. The elation I felt at that moment was almost indescribable. Have you ever watched the Robert Redford movie, *The Natural*, when he hits that home run into the lights to win the big game near the end of the film? That's what it was like for me. I suppose I should have acted more nonchalant, as if I had done this many times, but I couldn't help myself. I went on to hit a triple and a double in that closing game, but that didn't compare to my one and only home run.

Each year for five years I had worked harder than the year before to become a better baseball player, to prove to myself and others that I was their equal. I had gone from mascot to team leader and from obscure shyness to outgoing top-performing player. It doesn't get any better than that. I remember thinking to myself that after my performance during that final game I would no longer have to prove myself to others ever again. I had arrived. Or so I thought.

Chapter Four

New Challenges

"The will is more important than the skill when it comes to scaling a wall."

– Robert Schuller

New Challenges

In 1963 Dad had purchased a good-sized residential lot in the Belmont Shore area of Long Beach and had begun construction on a custom home that he and Mom designed themselves. His real estate and construction activities were expanding and thriving, so he wanted to build our family a larger home. There had been a fairly decent-sized main house situated at the front of the lot on Prospect Avenue, but it had recently been razed by a fire. A smaller guest house in back and a free-standing garage escaped damage.

Because we were soon going to live in a different part of town, Kirk, Brian and I needed to change schools. The new school year was going to start in September of 1963. Our new home wouldn't be completed until April or May of 1964, so Dad drove Kirk and me to our new junior high school, Will Rogers, and Brian to a nearby Catholic school located in Belmont Heights each morning. Dad didn't want us to transfer mid-year.

I had not exactly enjoyed much of my social interaction while at Hill Junior High School. I felt that except during baseball games I had been a bit passive, tended to be a people pleaser and just tried to get along with my classmates which didn't always work out as I hoped. As a result, I now decided to alter my persona at Rogers. I thought I needed to toughen up my image, be more aloof and keep to myself. I wore Levi's, pointed "pixie-boots" that were popular shoes with kids at the time (unless you were an athlete), plaid, woolen Pendleton shirts and combed my tonic-oiled hair back on the sides to look more menacing.

I actually thought this nonsense was going to keep me from being teased, dissed, or picked on and would basically be left alone. I looked like Pat Boone in Elvis Presley's clothes. It's true that I was physically larger and stronger as I entered eighth grade, but I still wore glasses, looked a little awkward and oh, yeah, I was still missing a left hand. As for acting tough, my new classmates saw right through me because I didn't perform that act well and I tended to revert back to my old ways. I have never met anyone in my life who didn't like my mother, ever. While I can't claim that about myself I do share some of her kinder, gentler qualities that made me more likable than the tough guy I tried to portray. My plan was foiled by my own actions, and thankfully so.

Rogers Junior High had a different feel to it than Hill right from the start. It's hard to explain, but it felt and looked like a mini-mid-western college campus, because it had been built many years ago and wasn't "modern." The students there were much friendlier to one another and there were fewer cliques. There were cliques, of course, but not as many. I was mostly treated much better there than I had been at Hill, once I stopped trying to hang out with the smokers and the honest-to-goodness tough guys, or so they thought. That wasn't me.

The first day of school at Rogers, Paul Hartman, a likeable guy and as it turned out a very good athlete, came up to me and asked me if I played baseball and if I was a pitcher. He said he read a newspaper article about me recently and was impressed. I told him I didn't think the article was about me as I had never been aware of such an article, but that didn't keep him from striking up a friendship with me that lasted for many years.

One disappointing outcome of our move to Belmont Shore was that I was now out of the district where I would have been eligible to play baseball in the Los Altos Pony League as I had hoped the year before. Now that my skills had been elevated I had really thought I could compete at that level and felt I needed to if I was going to play baseball in high school, which I thought I wanted to do when the time came.

In the fall I tried out for the Rogers eighth-grade flag-football team and made it onto the squad. I played on the defensive line and did fairly well. Not great, but I was somewhat satisfied with my overall performance. In one of the games my dang glasses kept sliding down my nose and after a particular play I made the unforgivable mistake of calling time out to put them on the bench. You only get a certain number of time outs in each half and coaches usually want to keep them for more important reasons than a player's loose glasses. Redemption is a wonderful thing, however. On the very next play the other team had to punt. The ball was snapped and I brushed through the blocker in front of me and I stretched out my right arm just as the punter kicked the football. I blocked his punt and to everyone on the sidelines it looked as though I had somehow done so with my head. Everyone cheered. We got the ball and scored, winning the game by seven points.

Even the coach praised my gallant efforts and completely forgot about my calling time out inappropriately. The ninth graders praised me as well. That was a big deal. Ninth graders didn't usually give eighth graders the time of day. The season ended with me gaining respect from my teammates and others and life was good at Rogers Junior High School.

On a chilly Friday morning in Dallas, Texas, at 11:40 AM on November 22, 1963 at Love Field, America's mostly popular, young and seemingly vibrant President, John Fitzgerald Kennedy and his beautiful wife, Jacqueline arrived with their aides and entourage aboard Air Force One following a short flight from Carswell Air Force Base in Fort Worth. Kennedy had come to Texas to deliver a breakfast speech to the Fort Worth Chamber of Commerce; followed by a luncheon speech at the Dallas Assembly and Science Research Center. He was also to give a dinner speech that evening at the Dallas Municipal Auditorium and then had expected to spend a weekend of relaxation at Vice-President Lyndon Johnson's expansive Texas ranch. Destiny intervened.

There has been a virtual plethora of accounts of what transpired following the Fort Worth breakfast speech during the motorcade through Dallas that fateful day, so there is no need to recap the story here. The Kennedy Assassination and its aftermath slapped America out of its naiveté and innocence of the time to come face-to-face with the numerous serious challenges and divides that permeated the United States and the world. Depicted by the media almost from day one of the Kennedy Administration to be "Camelot," which was far more myth than fact, it did not change many people's belief in a new day and greater possibilities for Americans; until the shots rang out.

I was in Wood-Shop Class The morning of November 22, 1963 Our instructor came out of his office and told us the news that President Kennedy had been shot. We didn't know any details. It's one thing to read historical accounts about the assassination of Abraham Lincoln, and Presidents Garfield and McKinley, but quite another to be witnessing it, albeit via radio accounts. Upon getting home that day and for many days and weeks thereafter, that is all that we watched on television or talked about at school. It was such a terrible thing to happen to Kennedy, his family and our nation. Personally, with few exceptions between then and now (the Reagan years for example) I believe our country has not been as strong, secure or confident since. That will only change for the positive with real leadership and a return to adherence to our Constitution as intended by our Founders.

One of the other reasons that life was good at Rogers was the friendship I enjoyed with Monica Cosenza. Monica was one of the most outgoing, beautiful and kindest girls I had ever known up to that point. She was as popular as anyone in our entire school. Despite being so popular, she treated me as if I were just as admired as she was and "belonged" in her sphere. All she had to do was say, "Hi Lynn," and smile that gorgeous smile and I melted away. Monica Cosenza-Brady still has a heart of gold and she remains a gorgeous girl to this day, even though she is now a grandmother; a very proud grandmother, I might add. We remain in contact on a regular basis. She was and is a very positive influence on me. I am truly blessed to still have her as my friend.

Another wonderful friend from Rogers who remains close to my heart is Patti Gehrke. When we moved into the home Dad built in Belmont Shore, Patti was one of my neighbors, living just around the corner from us. She was and is one of the kindest, most generous and warm-hearted individuals I have ever known. She also has a great, contagious laugh that is stimulated quite easily, especially by a class clown. While I didn't have any serious girlfriends while at Rogers I enjoyed the company of numerous young ladies, none of whom were as sweet to me as Patti. Another positive influence on me while in my teens, Patti is a special friend, indeed.

During gym class in the fall we also played flag football. My athletic ability had improved to the point where I was now a captain selecting the players in pick-up games rather than waiting to be the last guy standing when I was younger. I played quarterback on my team because I knew football strategy better than those who were typically on my team, could throw the ball accurately and because I was good running with the ball, too. I had also learned to be more aggressive, at least on the playing field. This came in handy one day with a kid on an opposing team. He was older than we were, because he had flunked the previous year and was a troublemaker. He pushed a smaller teammate of mine to the ground and laughed at him as he walked away. Sensitive to being bullied or seeing others mistreated, I walked up behind this jerk and kicked him in the ass as hard as I could. This guy was much bigger than I was but I didn't care. I wanted justice. I yelled at him and told him never to do that again to any of my teammates. He knew I meant it and backed away. I was actually a little startled at my actions and the outcome, but quite pleased with myself for having stood up to this bully. I was never afraid to do so again in my life. I even considered bringing a banana to school with me again (just kidding).

In the spring I tried out for baseball and made the team, but my heart wasn't in it like it once had been. I hadn't practiced anywhere near as much as I should have and I felt a little rusty. I'm not sure if it was because I didn't get to play Pony League as I had once hoped, the lousy fields we now played on, the different players, growing distractions such as my heightened interest in girls (did I mention Monica Cosenza and Patti Gehrke?) or something else. It just wasn't as much fun. Another factor was that the baseball coach had never really seen me play before and even though I was performing fairly well for him he seemed to believe that my skills were not comparable to those of my teammates. I knew that was baloney, but he was the coach. I ended up playing very little. All in all it turned out to be a forgettable baseball season.

As I entered the ninth grade I began to be much more interested in football than baseball. The NFL was gaining in popularity ever since NBC televised nationally on December 28, 1958 what has widely become known as "The Greatest Football Game Ever Played"; the 1958 National Football League Championship Game played between the Baltimore Colts and the New York Giants.

The final score of the 1958 Championship game was Baltimore, 23 and New York, 17. This was the first overtime game ever played during an NFL championship. The drama of this game was palpable and it began a journey by the NFL to becoming more popular than Major League Baseball, "America's Pastime," which had been the number one sport in the nation for decades.

I watched a lot of football after that eventful championship contest, especially in the early and mid-'60s. I idolized many great players, but there was one particular player I admired the most. He was the fastest, strongest, most punishing running back I had and have ever seen. Jim Brown, fullback for the Cleveland Browns, epitomized what a professional football player should be; Intelligent, tough, fast and strong. Nobody seemed to be able to bring him down, at least not by themselves. He was remarkable. He led the league in rushing in eight of his nine seasons in the NFL. He remains the only rusher in NFL history to average over 100 yards per game! No one has ever impressed me more on a football field than Jim Brown; No one.

I played in a lot of pick-up football games on the weekends as well as playing in gym class and in intramurals. I watched every football game I could, which back then was far fewer than the over-saturated air waves that today seem to televise professional and college games on a multitude of channels nearly every day of the week. Heck, there wasn't even Monday Night Football yet!

At the end of the first or second week of school in ninth grade a bunch of us guys went to the annual Milk Bowl at Veterans Stadium in northeast Long Beach near Long Beach City College and the Douglas Aircraft plant.

New Challenges

The Milk Bowl was a charity event held each year to raise money for the school lunch program for needy kids within the Long Beach Unified School District. Each of the six high school teams in the Moore League; Wilson, Poly, Millikan, Lakewood, Jordan and Downey played two quarter-length football "games" on the Saturday afternoon prior to the season starting. It was like the "Carnival" I had experienced each year in Little League Baseball. It was very stimulating to be there, to see the players up close, and to feel the excitement of high school football.

I didn't make the squad on the ninth-grade flag-football team. The coach felt that other players had outperformed me in tryouts and inter-squad games, so he cut me. I was not a happy camper, but I had to be honest with myself and admit that I had not put forth the required effort since I knew I needed to work harder than my teammates to be on an even par with them due to my perceived "handicap." I had done myself a disservice by expecting to make the team rather than working hard to do so. I had no one to blame but myself.

A fortuitous visit to an Optimist Club breakfast meeting with Dad and Kirk during the summer prior to going to high school helped to further ignite my interest in playing football. The guest speaker that morning was Eddie Meador, the free safety for the Los Angeles Rams who would go on to have an outstanding career, being named to the Pro-Bowl six times. After Meador's presentation Dad told him that I wanted to play football in high school and asked him if he had any advice for me. Meador replied, "Volunteer to be first in the drills, do exactly as your coach instructs you to do, work harder than your teammates and always go the extra mile." Those words, coming from an NFL player, stuck with me for years and would help me to achieve important goals in the future.

Upon graduation from junior high school there were a number of us who wanted to try out for football in high school. Other than junior high flag football, I had never played organized football but because my friends were going to try out I wanted to as well. A few of my friends had older brothers who played in high school and were all great guys who were highly respected.

The varsity football program at Long Beach Woodrow Wilson High School where we would be attending in the fall was a well-organized, successful program that had a long winning tradition. Many Wilson players earned football scholarships to great schools, such as USC, UCLA, Stanford, Cal, the University of Oregon, Arizona State and others. It was considered an honor and a privilege to play football at Wilson. Right or wrong I saw that the varsity football players were the most respected guys on campus. Knowing how much they were admired I made up my mind that come hell or high water by the time I was a senior at Wilson High School I would play varsity football. I felt a burning desire to achieve that goal to be among those guys and to hopefully be as admired and respected as any of them.

I was going to attend high school with many kids I already knew from Hill Junior High who hadn't exactly held me in high esteem, and many other kids I didn't know from the other junior high schools that fed students to Wilson. I knew how difficult the high school experience could be for some people. I also wanted to play football to gain respect right from the start of our sophomore year to avoid feeling like an outsider or someone who wasn't "in." That was perhaps a bit shallow, but I had developed a pretty strong desire to be liked rather than dissed. There were over 4,000 baby-boomer students who would be attending Wilson and I wanted to be accepted by as many of them as possible. A "big man on campus" I didn't expect to be, but I sure wanted to hang out with them. I was motivated. Maybe for some of the wrong reasons at that point, but motivated nonetheless.

Those of us who were planning on going out for football started running and lifting weights in the summer to get into shape and ready for tryout camp in early September. Dad had recently purchased a set of weights for me; barbells and dumbbells so I could work out at home. I did curls, which is an exercise where you hold the barbell in both hands with your palms up and spread out to the width of your shoulders, then "curl" the weights from down across your legs below your waist, up to your chest and back down. I did several repetitions of this exercise, usually ten. You might be asking yourself, "How did he do curls with only one hand?" I'll explain:

I held the barbell with my right hand and balanced it near the end of my left arm, resting on my little thumb. I held the barbell a little closer to the left end rather than equidistant from each of the weights attached near the ends of the bar so that the bulk of the weight was on the right side. I then just curled the barbell up with my right arm. The barbell would slip down from my little thumb to the bend of my arm as I curled the bar upward, imitating the action of my right arm. It would slip gently back down against my thumb as I brought the bar back down. This simulated a "normal" curl rather closely and ensured that I was exercising both arms in this way. A little rough on my little thumb, but effective.

Another exercise I did was the overhead or military press. In this exercise you hold the barbell in both hands with your palms down, holding it tight with your arms up against your chest. Then you push or press the barbell straight up above your head until your arms are outstretched and your elbows are close to locking, and then bring the weights back down to your starting position. This exercise didn't mess up my little thumb, but it was a bit of a precarious maneuver. In my left arm there are two bones, just like everyone else, the Ulna and the Radius. The Ulna is slightly longer than the Radius, so I could actually rest the barbell on the very top of the Ulna up against the top of the Radius, and up against my chest after essentially flipping the barbell up onto the Ulna; An interesting maneuver and a bit unsteady as I mentioned, but I never dropped the barbell doing this exercise. Thank goodness.

The bench press exercise that I did was much the same technique as the military press, except that lying on my back with the barbell stretched across my chest I would slip my left arm under the barbell and grab it with my right hand, then simply push straight up... carefully, very carefully. I never had a spotter, which wasn't very smart, but the maximum weight was only 110 pounds, so I thought it wouldn't be necessary. Only one time did I ever have the barbell slip off my left arm. Fortunately I was able to quickly push it up with my right arm and turned my head just enough to have the bar hit the bench underneath me instead of my head, which wouldn't have felt too good, even at 110 pounds. I did however, have the weights slip off the left end of the bar a couple times because I failed to tighten that side's screw enough, and because the bar was uneven at the apex of the lift since my right arm is longer than my left. Lesson finally learned.

As you might imagine, I was later thrilled when they came out with the Universal Weight Machine that eliminated the need to use barbells when lifting weights. Halleluiah!

Running on our own during the summer before football training camp began helped get us into shape, but it would soon became apparent after camp started that we did not run anywhere near enough. Many more challenges would soon present themselves as I prepared to enter high school and attend summer football camp at Woodrow Wilson High School.

Chapter Five

Learning to Apply the *Power* of Perseverance

"I do not think there is any other quality so essential to success of any kind as the quality of perseverance. It overcomes almost anything, even nature."

– John D. Rockefeller

Learning to Apply the *Power* of Perseverance

HIGH SCHOOL TWO-A-DAY SUMMER FOOTBALL training camp began at the peak of the summer heat in 1965, just a couple of weeks prior to the opening day of school. In high school back then there were three categories of high school football teams: varsity; junior varsity, and what was referred to as the "B" team. The varsity team, of course, was comprised of the best football players at the school. It was made up of mostly juniors and seniors who possessed a high level of strength, agility, talent, skill and knowledge of the game. The junior varsity also included talented players who were juniors and sophomores, but either didn't have the requisite size, skills or strength required to be on the varsity or there just hadn't been room on the roster for them. The "B" team would today typically be referred to as the "Freshman Team," except that juniors and even seniors could qualify to play on the B team if they had the correct "exponents." These exponents were measurements derived by combining a player's age, height and weight. Any combination of total points, or exponents that put your total over the limit meant that you would be ineligible to play on the B team, so you would then have to go out for either the junior varsity or varsity teams.

In other words, if you were 14 instead of 15, you could weigh a little more or be taller than the limit and still play on the B team. You could also be 16 or even 17 years old and still qualify if your height or weight were below the maximum allowed. I was a little taller at five-foot-eight and a little heavier at 165 pounds than the maximums allowed, but because my 15th birthday wasn't until

November 5th my exponent totals qualified me for participation on the B team. I wouldn't have made the weight requirement had I not dieted for several weeks prior to our "weigh-in" day when we were officially designated as eligible or not to play on the B team. Not only did I diet, on the day of official weigh-in I stripped down beyond my underwear to be as light as possible, much to the surprise of the other players and the coaches. They understood, apparently, because they said nothing. Naked, I made it. If I had a left hand that little bit of "extra" weight would have disqualified me; in this case, "different" was good! This was important to me because although I was determined to play varsity football by the time I was a senior, I not played organized tackle football or even worn football equipment before going to high school, which put me at a disadvantage from all those guys who had played Pop Warner Football. I was determined to play varsity by my senior year, but I was also realistic.

I could have gone out for the junior varsity team as many of my classmates did, but I truly believed that I would have a much better chance of playing if I was on the B team. And I needed playing time to reach my ultimate goal. But even playing on the B team required that you actually make the squad. If you weren't good enough you would be cut from the team, as I had been in ninth grade. I wasn't going to make the same mistake I had made back then. I would leave nothing to chance with respect to putting out maximum effort. While my desire to make the team was high, my skill level was not and I didn't even know what position to go out for. That decision was soon made for me.

Coach Morton was a huge man who stood about six-foot, six-inches tall and had played briefly for the San Francisco 49ers. He and Coach Mertz, his assistant, decided that because of my relative size and "other" factors, the best position for me would be offensive tackle. Now, I had played center, guard and tackle in pick-up football games when I was younger, but in junior high school I had been a quarterback, running back and even wide receiver in gym class and intramurals. That was much more fun. I wasn't that wild about being a lineman... not that there's anything wrong with that. I just thought I'd rather play a more glamorous position. But I didn't rock the boat. I went where they told me to go.

The entire group of prospects from each level trained together for the first several days, so players who would ultimately be on the varsity, junior varsity and the B teams were all practicing together by position; linemen, backs, and receivers. This was the first time I had ever seen the types of drills we were put through. Some were easier than others. We had no helmets, shoulder pads or other equipment yet, just shorts, T-shirts and football cleats. The first thing we were required to do was get into a three-point stance. This is an elementary part of the game requiring you to first spread your feet out to approximately shoulder width or a little more. On the command by the coach yelling, "Ready-set," you put your hands on your knees. Then on the command, "Down," you got into the three-point stance by dropping your right foot a step behind your left foot (unless you were left-handed, which, of course I'm not), and then putting your right hand down to the ground, resting it with your thumb stretched outward to the left and on the knuckles of your first two fingers of the right hand. Your left forearm would then rest on your left knee; Simple.

"Ready-set... down," went the coach's command. Then he would say, "Up," and we would get ready to repeat this. We repeated it over and over again, and again. Then we'd be down in the three-point stance and coach would yell, "Now hold that position." We'd stay down until he yelled, "Up!" We did this each day that summer for quite a while. It taught us discipline and how to do this in unison; as a team.

Another thing we were taught early on was how to get into what was called the "hitting position." All actions in football start from the hitting position. This requires you to spread your feet out to be about shoulder width or slightly wider pointing straight ahead. You bend at the hips, leaning forward a bit with your head and eyes up looking straight ahead, with your arms bent out in front of you and your fists clenched. Whenever a coach would yell, "Hit," you were required to immediately get into the hitting position. From this point you would start many different drills.

One of the early drills we did was to come out from the line we were in and face the presiding coach. He then commanded us to get into the hitting position and then upon another signal from him, we were to start pumping our legs running in place, at a quick pace; the coach would then yell, "left," or right, and we would do a quarter turn, hopefully in the correct direction. This didn't look too tough. When it was my turn to step forward from my line and perform the drill, I got into place and the coach yelled,

"Hit!" I immediately got into the hitting position. When coach said, "Go," I started pumping my legs, except when I first did it as my legs pumped up and down my feet turned outward. I looked like a duck on a hot plate.

"Point your feet straight ahead, rookie," barked the coach. So I did my best to do so. When it was my turn again to perform this drill (we all repeated each drill several times), I got into the hitting position and when coach yelled, "hit," my legs began pumping again. Daffy Duck had returned. "Point your feet straight ahead, I said," the coach yelled, clearly not amused. That night I practiced this one at home while facing a floor-length mirror until Daffy disappeared.

Another drill required us to get into the hitting position and on command spring forward and do a somersault about five yards ahead, then once up on our feet run for about ten more yards. This was done to help teach us how to go to the ground and come up running to be able to make a block, or tackle the ball carrier. I did this without a problem. At least without gear on it was no problem.

There were a number of other drills that basically tested your coordination, strength, speed and stamina. Some were easy and some weren't. All of them eventually tired you out and made you sore because you were using muscles you rarely used. One of the toughest of these drills was called the "Lombardi Drill," named for the legendary NFL coach who invented it. In this drill you got into the hitting position and on the command started running in place. When the coach yelled "Down," you dropped to the grass prone onto your hands and torso. Then you had to bounce back upright immediately and return to running in place. This was one of the most strenuous of all the drills, especially as the coach gradually picked up the pace of having you drop down and bounce back up.

We did many types of drills that first morning, then, just prior to the conclusion of practice we all ran wind sprints. We did ten or so of these that first morning. You come up to the goal line, get into a three-point stance on command, and when the coach yells, "Hut," you start running as fast as possible for 50 yards. Then you turn around and come back from whence you came. These are grueling after a long practice, and were especially so on the first day. You don't want to finish last if you are trying to make the team. You better be trying your best so you didn't get cut because the coaches thought you're either too slow or too lazy to play for them. I had to run my absolute fastest each and every time because I wasn't that fast. I was faster than most of the linemen, but not by a lot.

As I said, these were "two-a-day" practices. That meant we practiced in the morning for two hours or more and then returned in the afternoon to practice again. Several kids did not return on that first afternoon. But I did. I admit to thinking as we ran wind sprints that morning, "What did you get yourself into," but I came back anyway. After all, I had set a goal to one day play varsity football and quitting was not an option. Besides, the camaraderie was great. Being out there as a sophomore practicing with Wilson High School senior, varsity heroes like Ron Fujikawa, Terry Dekrai, Gil Powell, Doug McKenzie, Sid Smith, and juniors like Bob Grich, Jim Price, Dennis Dummit, John Kahler, Dale Nosworthy and Jeff Severson was very exciting and a boost to one's ego. Ron was quarterback and

Terry was a wide receiver. They were such a great tandem that they both had been named to the varsity All-League, All-City and All-CIF teams as juniors.

Many of these great athletes went on after their days at Wilson to achieve other successes. Ron Fujikawa went to Stanford and later became a judge. Sid Smith starred at USC and played several years in the NFL. Bob Grich was drafted by the Baltimore Orioles and later played for many years for the Southern California Angels baseball team. Dennis Dummit became a junior college All-American and went on to set numerous passing records at UCLA.

For the first couple of days we just did drills and ran wind sprints at the end of practice in our shorts and T-shirts. No pads yet. Boy was I sore the morning after our first few days of practice! The running I did over the summer barely helped. I came to learn that no matter how much you train on your own during the summer you rarely work yourself as hard as the coaches work you in practice. In the NFL in recent years you could find examples that are contrary to this, like Jerry Rice and Ladanian Tomlinson and others, but back in the day there were few athletes who worked that hard in the off-season.

On the last day of practice before we received our gear we were required to run a mile around the track in under six minutes. One of my new friends who had gone to Jefferson Junior High, Gordy McNeil, gave me advice prior to running the mile. "Jog in the turns and sprint in the straight-a-ways," he said. "That will help you conserve energy." That sounded reasonable to me. I had never been much of a long-distance runner. Heck, I didn't really like running short distances, either, unless I was playing baseball or football or doing some other activity that required it. When it was our group's turn to run, coach yelled, "Go," and we were off! Faster in the straight-a-ways and slower in the turns I ran the mile in just under the six-minute requirement. Those who did not had to run it each day until they beat the six-minute time. Some who didn't make the time on their first try simply did not come back.

We would soon get our gear and practice uniforms. I had improved some since that first day, ran the mile in the required time and was looking forward to the challenges ahead. On the day that we were given our football helmets, shoulder pads, hip pads, knee and thigh pads and the practice pants and jerseys, and then were assigned our lockers, I made a brilliant deduction as if I were Sherlock Holmes. It was a long process to hand out equipment to everyone, but exciting just the same because I was going to be a real-life football player with a helmet and pads and everything! Only one thing; when they handed me my helmet it had only one protective bar as my face "mask." I had watched a lot of football and the offensive and defensive linemen playing in the trenches, colliding with each other for four long quarters, often banging their heads together, had face masks that were called "cages" for good reason – multiple bars going up and down, and bars going across; A cage. When I looked at my helmet again and saw that lonely bar, which is the kind most place kickers wore, my deduction, my dear Watson, was that I probably wasn't expected to play much. How clairvoyant.

The drills became a little more difficult while wearing football equipment. For example, as we did our somersault drill the first several times, I tried to do it but ended up looking like a turtle that had been turned onto its back and couldn't get up; just a tad embarrassing? The pads were an issue as much as the helmet which made my head feel as heavy as an anvil, or so it seemed at first. I was only 14 and not that strong yet, but I eventually got the hang of it and felt more at ease as I was able to complete the maneuver like everyone else. Repetition is a wonderful thing.

With pads and helmets we also performed blocking and tackling drills. We did many different types of drills, over and over again, twice a day, with the ever-exhausting wind sprints that followed. We also simulated blocks against the "Blocking Sled," a steel contraption with wide metal protuberances covered with padding. There was an individual sled, a two-blocker sled and a five-blocker sled. There were several different drills utilizing these sleds, all designed to improve your blocking skills and to strengthen you as well.

A particularly aggressive and arduous drill was called the "Head-to-Head" drill. It was one of the toughest drills we practiced. In the head-to-head drill two blocking pads were set about three yards apart and one defensive lineman would face one offensive lineman in a face-off (head-to-head) in their three-point stance between the pads. A ball carrier, who was actually another lineman, which some of us referred to as a "tackling dummy," would stand behind the offensive lineman with the football tucked under one arm waiting for the coach's command to begin the drill. The design of the drill was for the coach to yell "Hut," and then the two linemen would collide while the running back (the ball carrier) tried to run past the defensive lineman between the two blocking pads and "score."

The offensive lineman was usually instructed to try to block the defender in one direction or the other, but not always. The more aggressive of the two linemen generally "won" this drill. If the defender won, the ball carrier got tackled... hard.

This drill often separated the men from the boys, so to speak. If you were quick off the ball, strong and aggressive, and not the least bit afraid of hard contact, you would be successful as the lineman, no matter if you were on defense or offense. The tougher, stronger and quicker you were, the better you were at this intense drill. I was quick off the ball, but not strong enough or aggressive enough to win very often. I gave all I had or thought I had on each drill, but knew I wasn't a top performer. The best thing I did during this drill was when I was the ball carrier. I discovered that most of the defenders, even the senior players, of which there were only a few, had a hard time tackling me. There was a message in there for future consideration.

It was very hot with all that equipment on except during the early morning workouts. The training sessions were extremely strenuous, but again, being out there on a football field among all these guys was also exhilarating! And it was made more so by knowing that only some of the boys coming to Wilson from their respective junior high schools even came to try outs and training camp. There were only a select few students out of thousands who would play football in 1965 for Woodrow Wilson High School. We felt like a collective group of elite students.

We were also given playbooks during training camp and told to study each play so we would memorize our specific assignments and be ready in a couple of days to start running through them. The plays were in the form of the famous "Xs and Os," drawn in many formation combinations, such as the well-known T-formation with the two halfbacks and the fullback in the backfield in line behind the quarterback and guards, and the pro formation with only the fullback and left halfback in the backfield and the right halfback or "flanker" split off the tight end at various distances.

Our offensive plays were fairly easy to remember because they had names rather than numbers. Instead of 32-Sweep or 28-Power Trap, our plays had names like Bull and Batter or Jar and Jolt. If the play's name had an "R" in it the play went to the right. If it had an "L" in its name we ran it to the left. Our coaches called this the "KISS" method: Keep It Simple Stupid. It was their way of making things less complicated.

Unfortunately for me, while the naming system was simple, I was closer to stupid when it came to memorizing the blocking assignments for an offensive tackle. They went something like this: "Man on my nose block him, if no man on my nose block the first lineman to your right (or left), if no lineman on your right (or left) go through the line and block the linebacker or the first person you come into contact with." These assignments really weren't that complicated, but I thought they were at the time or maybe I just had a mental block, making them seem more complicated than they actually were. Or maybe I just didn't want to be a lineman. What tended to complicate them for me were the multiple formations from which they were run that could change each play assignment a bit. You had to be very aware of which formation you were in to know just who to block; T-formation, single-wing, pro-formation, etc.

When we broke up into our specific teams, varsity, junior varsity and the B team, we practiced as a unit. We did the drills and ran plays. At first we ran the plays without any defenders at all, and then we ran them against defenders holding blocking bags and had to block the defenders as our assignments indicated. We would repeat each play time and time again to get everyone in sync. If someone blew an assignment we'd run the play over. If you blew an assignment more than once or couldn't recite your specific assignment word-for-word you got on Coach Mertz's "Brown List" and had to run a lap around the field. The "Brown" was synonymous with s - - t, so you didn't want to get on that list. I rarely did.

Scrimmages were like mini-games played between our own teammates. No blocking bags were used. They replicated game conditions to the extent that they could and gave us all a taste of what it was like to block and tackle live, under fire. In a scrimmage the coaches can stop the action and instruct the players what to do, how to correct mistakes, demonstrate better blocking or tackling techniques and so forth. It is a valuable part of training leading up to your first game.

A few days before training camp broke and school started the coaches made their decisions on the depth chart, meaning who would start at each offensive and defensive position, and who would be second string, third string on down if there were more players. The "deeper" you were on the depth chart the less likely you were to play very much. Had I been any deeper on the right offensive tackle depth chart my spot would have been labeled, "abyss." My earlier Sherlock Holmes-like deduction was seemingly accurate. But at least I wasn't cut from the team, as a few others had been.

As the 1965 football season began our team was expected to do well. The Wilson High B Team had won the Moore League Title several years in a row and there was every reason to believe that we would repeat that accomplishment this year. As it turned out, we did just that, beating our non-conference opponents handily each and every week, and then our conference opponents as well, even our cross-town rival, Poly High School. We were 9-0 at season's end, an undefeated team. The other Moore League schools we beat soundly included Lakewood, Millikan, Downey and Jordan. Our team outscored all of our non-conference and conference opponents by a total of 161 points. The coaches were so proud of our team that they had mentioned that they intended to award each and every player with a school letter for their letterman's jackets because we became Moore League Champions.

Now, I went to every practice, often early. I worked hard in practice to be worthy of playing in the games and hoped that I would get my chance to prove that I was going to be a good football player and a valuable member of the team who would contribute to our success. And we won so many games by huge margins I thought surely that the coaches would allow even *me* to play in a game or two without jeopardizing victory and our shot at winning the league title.

Oh, I did get to play alright... but it wasn't until the last quarter of the last game of my sophomore season, reminiscent of my two-year stint on the Braves in Little League several years earlier. The coaches were eventually dissuaded from giving every member of the B team a school letter. It was determined that only those team members who had distinguished themselves on the field of play deserved to be awarded school letters. That was and is as it should be. You should not diminish the hard-won achievements of some by also rewarding those who do not truly deserve to be rewarded.

Other than surviving training camp, making the team, being able to hang out with guys who were among the most respected and admired within a student body of more than 4,000 students, gaining the respect of juniors and seniors who actually played in the games, as well as my teammates who were also sophomores, and learning the game better (and these were all significant), there was only one stand-out experience of that season that I'd like to share with you.

In that final quarter of the last game of my first year in high school football I was put into the game at right defensive tackle. I hadn't even really trained to be a defensive player, but I could have cared less. I was getting a chance to play! The field was muddy because it had rained the day before our game against Lakewood High School. I was in on the tackle of one of their running backs. It was a big pile-up. The jerseys we wore in games on the B team were old hand-me-downs from the varsity of the late 1950s and the sleeves were three-quarter length. My jersey was wet and muddy and the left sleeve fell down over the end of my left arm. Just as I was pulling myself up I got this terrific idea (I thought so anyway). I stood up, grabbed my left arm and started shouting, "My hand, my hand... where's my hand?"

I looked around and saw the referee. I thought he was going to swallow his whistle. I considered my actions in this regard to be hilarious (class clown, remember), but I don't think he shared my timing or sense of humor. Anyway, that was the most significant occurrence of that unremarkable season. At least it was unremarkable for me.

When the season was long over I reflected upon all that had transpired that year. I made up my mind that if I was going to achieve my goal of playing varsity football by the time I was a senior, and I was driven and determined to do so, more now than ever, I was going to have to work even harder than before. And since I was going to put forth the kind of effort I believed it would take to make the junior varsity team next season I was also going to choose for myself what position I would play. I remembered clearly how hard I had been to bring down as the ball carrier in the head-to-head drills. Knowing that running backs get to score touchdowns and bask in more glory than a typical lineman, the position I decided to play was fullback, like my idol, Jim Brown.

Chapter Six

—

The Year of the Underdog

"It is time for us all to stand up and cheer the doer, the achiever — the one who recognizes the challenge and does something about it."

— Vince Lombardi

The Year of the Underdog

FOLLOWING THE 1965 FOOTBALL SEASON I worked on my studies and was actually earning mostly A's and B's. I liked my classes and most of my teachers at Wilson and that helped raise my enthusiasm for doing well. One of my favorite classes was Print Shop. We learned how to use a commercial printing press, bind books and other things related to printing. But the activity I enjoyed the most was setting type. In the "old" days, printers had to set type into words, sentences and paragraphs in order to print anything, like books, newspapers... anything. And they had to set type by hand. Originally printers used wooden type, but in more "modern" times the individual letters and punctuation marks were made out of lead. My instructor thought this was going to be too much of a challenge for me and suggested that I do special projects instead so I didn't have to set type like the other students. Inside, I was not happy. I also thought to myself, "Here we go again," and politely said to my instructor that I would prefer to try it first, if he wouldn't mind? I was outwardly respectful, but inside I was saying to myself, "Yes I can, yes I will, just watch me!"

I became the fastest, most accurate type-setter in my particular class, much to the amazement of the instructor and in no small way to my personal amusement. I'm not saying it was easy, because it wasn't. I had to be creative, and compared to lifting 110 pounds of weights over my head, it wasn't that difficult either.

During the summer between my sophomore and junior years at Wilson High I decided to do more than just run around on my own in preparation for the upcoming season and my attempt to play fullback on the junior varsity team. I began lifting weights more frequently than in the past, ran wind sprints, laps around the football field and ran up and down the football stadium steps. I did this on a regular basis. There was time for going to the beach (we lived only a couple of blocks from great beaches) and sailing as well, since Dad was heavily into sailboat racing by this time and Kirk and I joined him and others as his racing crew. However, I remained focused on the goal at hand.

I was also working most weekdays that summer with Kirk at Dad's construction site in Garden Grove where he was building an apartment complex and a strip center. We were essentially day laborers doing all manner of jobs such as painting, trash removal, carrying lumber from apartment to apartment and anything else that needed to be done. It was hard work but it helped me get into shape, in addition to instilling in me a strong work ethic; I would need it if I was to make the junior varsity team and play fullback, which was my next goal and by far my biggest personal challenge to date.

When football training camp commenced in the summer of 1966 I was in very good shape, had grown another inch and weighed 175 pounds. My skills had improved noticeably over the past year. When we were told to line up in the positions we expected to play I lined up with the fullbacks. You should have been there to see the look on the faces of nearly all the players and especially the coaches when they saw where I had lined up. Running backs with two hands fumble the football. There just weren't very many one-handed running backs in the country, if any at that time. I didn't think the coaches were in a hurry to have one on their team, either. No matter.

Some of my teammates even tried to dissuade me from going out for fullback. I would have none of it. I had made up my mind and I was sticking to my decision, win, lose or draw. I knew what I wanted and that didn't include going back to the offensive line. It was clear that I would be an underdog, but hadn't I watched and read about countless underdogs who persevered against difficult odds and more? I certainly had and I knew it wasn't an impossible dream to achieve my goal. It was improbable maybe, but not impossible.

One of the junior varsity coaches, Ewing H. "Bill" Crutchfield, was a well-respected teacher and coach. He was also a former World War II Marine Corp pilot who was a hero in the war having been shot down twice in enemy territory. He later served as a spotter for fellow pilots in the Philippines behind enemy lines. Coach Crutchfield had also been a star baseball player at USC after the war and was drafted by a major league baseball team, only to suffer a broken leg sliding into second base, which ended his baseball career prematurely. Coach seemingly took a personal interest in me. He respected my desire to play fullback despite the natural doubts and concerns of others and worked with me not only during practice but sometimes before practice and even after practice to help me learn the position.

Just as in the previous year, we went through the same training schedule; first doing drills in shorts, T-shirts and cleats, then the one-mile run under six minutes.

When we were given our helmets, pads, practice pants and jerseys, and assigned our lockers, lo and behold, this time my helmet had the standard face mask of a running back; two bars and a metal loop that would better help protect my nose. A good sign, I hoped.

While the drills were every bit as grueling as the previous year, I could execute them better and with more confidence this time around. No "Daffy Duck" and no upended turtle, for example. And the wind sprints were just as exhausting as before, but I was faster and kept pace with all but the fastest running backs. But the best part was that I was having fun while working as hard as I could to prove myself worthy of playing fullback, and I mean *playing*. I had no intention of simply being a fullback in practice and becoming nothing more than a spectator on game day.

With Coach Crutchfield's help and growing confidence in myself I began feeling comfortable running plays from the fullback position. With a year under my belt I also had no trouble clearly understanding my assignments on every play from each formation. Ironically, my stint as an offensive tackle made me a better blocker than most of the other running backs because all I had done in practice on the B team had been blocking, albeit on the line instead of from the running back position. Everything happens for a reason. But, then I committed what I thought was an egregious mistake that I feared might scuttle my progress. I fumbled the ball during a scrimmage at one of the afternoon practices while running an off-tackle play. A fumble was bad for any running back But I wasn't "any" running back. I was ticked at myself big time.

When I returned to the offensive huddle I was noticeably mad at myself. Coach Crutchfield looked me straight in the eye and asked, "Son, you didn't fumble the ball on purpose, did you?" I replied that I had not, so he then said, "Alright, just don't do it again and forget about it."

That was it. No scolding or admonishment. No look of incredulousness or any hint that I might be moved to a less critical position – just a cool, calm response and encouragement from an experienced, tough coach who empathized with his young players. Mr. Crutchfield knew which players to yell at, which to pat on the back, and which to kick in the butt. He knew I would respond best to reason and support as opposed to scolding and rebuke. I gained even more respect for Coach Crutchfield following that episode.

When the depth chart came out, there I was listed as the number two fullback behind Larry Newbill. I was also listed number two behind Larry on defense in the rover/monster or outside linebacker position. I was ecstatic! Not the starter, but close, very close. I knew I wasn't going to ride the pine this season! All that hard work in the summer and in two-a-days had paid off, or so I thought. In fact, during one of our practices leading up to our first non-conference game Larry had been making some mistakes and our head coach, Russell Jordan, yelled at Larry. He told him to get his act together because he didn't want to start me on both offense and defense; a sign that I was performing well.

Another fullback then emerged out of the blue who shall go nameless here. This student had been a fullback on the B team the previous year and had performed well when he played. He was a little faster and stronger than me, but, our understanding was that he was ineligible to play football as a junior. He had messed up his conduct grades at the end of our sophomore year, despite having a 3.5 scholastic grade-point average. His unsatisfactory conduct in certain classes made his overall conduct grade average fall below the CIF (California Interscholastic Federation) requirements. Ergo, he did not come out for the junior varsity team during the early part of summer training camp. But, and this is a BIG but, he somehow got one of his teachers from the previous year to change his final conduct grade from Unsatisfactory to Satisfactory. This raised his average up to the CIF minimum requirement. He was suddenly, "eligible."

I was naturally not happy in the least when this student came to practice and Coach Jordan placed him ahead of both Larry and me on the offensive depth chart. It was bad enough he hadn't been practicing with the team during the toughest sessions of two-a-days, but then to springboard past Larry and me was tough to take. I was now the number three fullback and my prospects for playing regularly had been greatly diminished. Getting a teacher to change your grade on a particular test or term paper or report because you misunderstood the assignment or were confused about a couple of test questions is one thing if you go back and are allowed to retake the test or improve your other work. Changing a grade to accommodate an athlete who was ineligible because of his own actions, even if it is "just" a conduct grade was and is wrong. It's not just about fairness, it's about integrity.

As the season progressed I continued to work hard and await my chance to play for the first time as a fullback in a game. While I had steadily improved and gained the respect of my teammates for my tenacity and efforts in practice, it wasn't until our second game when we played San Bernardino High School that I played. I was only in the game for a few offensive series and although I played okay it wasn't the kind of contribution to our winning the game that I had hoped for.

Our third game was against Chaffey High School in Ontario. We won the game by a score of 33-13. I played long and well enough that their head coach told Coach Crutchfield that as impressed as he was with our entire team's performance he was particularly surprised at how tough I had been as a blocker and while running with the football. When Mr. Crutchfield relayed that to me I was surprised to be singled out, but quite pleased.

My best game that season was against Downey High School, who we defeated in a shut-out 52-0. I carried the ball several times and averaged nearly four yards per carry. I scored a touchdown, my first one ever in high school! As usual Coach praised me for my blocking more than anything else, but he also said he was very happy for me to have scored one of our many touchdowns.

When we played Jordan High School on their field in North Long Beach I had another good game, again scoring a touchdown and gaining over 3.5 yards per carry. I can still see my friend, Gordy McNeil on one play racing down the right sideline after I helped to clear out the defenders by burying Jordan's left cornerback. Gordy was pretty fast and looked like he would score easily, but at the ten-yard line he tripped and fell short of the end zone. He never lived that down. We wouldn't let him. For years we reminded him about being tackled by the chalk line at the ten; Too funny! We won that game, too, another shutout by the score of 34 – 0. Following this game I was then moved back up the depth chart to second-string fullback. Larry was doing so well on defense that they wanted him to focus on playing rover.

Unfortunately, we tied instead of winning outright the final game of the season against Lakewood High School. We still won the Moore League Junior Varsity Championship title and preserved head coach, Russell Jordan's undefeated streak that now rose to 39 straight wins. In all we scored 242 points compared to that of 39 for all our opponents combined. It was an honor to play on that team with excellent players like Wes Edwards; Chris Key; Mark Lewis; Greg Sears; Jim Hunt; Dante Lobato (our speedy left halfback); Larry Newbill; Randy Stein; Bob McWhorter (who soon would be a medic in Vietnam); Jeff Burroughs (who would later become a proficient major league baseball player); Andy Orden (who later became a physician and co-host of *The Doctors* on television in 2008) and our starting quarterback, Dick Burdge (who went on to Yale). And there were other players like myself who made up for what they may have lacked in natural ability by working hard and playing within ourselves as a part of a strong team. These great guys included Jim Creighton; Pat Mathews; Kent Eastman; Gary Carter; Craig Weisenhutter; John Suttle; Mike Leininger; Jack Holland and many others. In fact, the trait that best characterized the B team in 1965 and this junior varsity team in 1966, both championship teams, was our collective teamwork.

The Year of the Underdog

I had come a long way in just one year. From having had no previous organized tackle football experience, to being put on the B team offensive line with one protective bar on my helmet, looking awkward and clumsy in drills and riding the bench, to making the '66 junior varsity team as a fullback (with Mr. Crutchfield's help), then playing well in games, blocking soundly enough to receive praise from my teammates, coaches and opposing coaches, and scoring touchdowns to help us win a championship. Needless to say I earned my JV Letter.

With all that I had accomplished on a personal level, including receiving no small amount of positive recognition from my peers, many of my teachers, other students throughout the school, my parents and my relatives, I wasn't totally satisfied with the outcome of my hard work. I had hoped to be the starting fullback so I would play more than I did. That opportunity eluded me, partly because of favoritism toward one particular player (who played quite well I must admit). I wasn't bitter or mad at Coach Jordan. I just knew I would have shown everyone, including myself, that I was better than I had been given credit for if I had more playing time under my belt. I am certain that I was not the only second or third-string football player who ever felt that way, and I wouldn't be the last. The good news was that it was my competitive spirit and my fierce determination to succeed that fueled those feelings. I vowed to turn disappointment into opportunity next year.

I was not a natural athlete and never a "star." I had to work extra hard to be taken seriously and to keep up with those who had superior skills and talent. And it *was* hard work. Summer training camp included grueling, hot, two-a-days, endless drills, wind sprints, the one-mile qualifying race, daily practices, studying the playbook, running and running play after play after play in practice, scrimmages, blocking and tackling... and the games themselves; not to mention keeping up with studies. But, I loved every second of it. I couldn't wait for the 1967 season to begin. I was just months away from achieving the major goal I had set for myself upon entering Wilson as a sophomore: To play varsity football by the time I was a senior.

Bring it on.

Chapter Seven

—

A Cinderella Team… Time to Be Bold

"One of the most difficult things everyone has to learn is that for your entire life you must keep fighting and adjusting if you hope to survive.
No matter who you are or what your position you must keep fighting for whatever it is you desire to achieve."

– George Allen

I SPENT MY SUMMER OF 1967 much as I had the previous year; working for Dad, going to the beach with friends, hanging out at 62nd Street and Woody's Goodies, the local snack shop. I also continued sailing and most importantly, lifting weights, running stadium steps, laps around the field, wind sprints, and pass patterns with other players who expected to play on the varsity football team in the fall. We had a brand new weight room at Wilson and I took full advantage of it. I lifted weights there as well as at home throughout the summer. I preferred the school weight room, however because it had Universal Weight Machines that enabled me to lift heavier weights without fear of cracking my cranium.

I was now 5-foot, 10-inches tall and weighed nearly 190 pounds. That's pretty good size for a high school fullback. I had wanted to get up to 200 pounds because fullbacks in the NFL nearly all weighed 200 pounds or more. I started drinking Nestles Instant Breakfast every morning and afternoon, but even with my workout regimen I was getting fat, not adding muscle, so I stopped. I got into great shape and in reality to have been any heavier would probably have slowed me down, which at 4.8 as my best-ever time in the 40-yard dash in high school, I couldn't afford to slow down.

Scott McKenzie, a terrific player we all respected and one of only two juniors who were called up to play varsity football during the 1966 season along with Randy Rossi, tried to convince me that I should be a guard instead of a fullback. He argued that because I was such an accomplished blocker while on the junior varsity I might play well enough at the guard position to be first string and maybe make the All-League and All-City teams. While that would have been a tremendous accomplishment and honor, I told Scott that I had already made up my mind. I would be a fullback once again.

He finally gave up pushing me in that direction one day when we played a touch football game at Wilson a couple of weeks before training camp began. I ran so well carrying the football that he came up to me after I had scored another touchdown (I scored three times that day) and said, "I didn't know you were that fast." I just smiled.

Even though I had played on the junior varsity the previous season, that fact alone didn't mean that I would automatically make the varsity squad. Things change, some obscure players mature into bigger, stronger, faster versions of their former selves and emerge like the beautiful butterfly from a lowly caterpillar. In addition, despite winning the 1966 Moore League Junior Varsity Championship and most all of us players from that team would be teammates on the varsity, the local sports writers were picking us to finish behind powerhouses, Long Beach Poly, Millikan and Lakewood. This meant that the coaches might be looking past this season ahead to the following season, essentially writing-off us seniors to groom the most talented juniors and develop their skills to have a better chance to win another championship the next year. I had to be prepared to work even harder than the past two years if I was going to make this team and play.

The varsity head coach, Owen Dixon, his offensive coordinator Gene "Skip" Rowland and defensive coach John Morton had seen me play on the junior varsity. They knew what to expect from me; I would give 100 percent all the time, because I had to. And they knew I was a very determined young man. That would be crucial to any chance I would have to make the team and contribute to its success.

Summer training camp took on a new atmosphere that was both exhilarating and humbling. On that first day in 1965 all of us sophomores had looked up to the juniors and especially the seniors as role models, respected athletes who had superior strength, speed, skills and talent. Not necessarily with envy (well, maybe a little), but certainly with admiration. The same was true in 1966, but some of my peers had already distinguished themselves beyond bench-warmer status in two previous seasons to emerge as solid players and even leaders in their own right. But this year, 1967, *we* were the seniors. The sophomores looked up to us much the same as we had looked up to our seniors two years ago. Most of the guys didn't let it affect them one way or the other, but I will admit that it fed my self-esteem and self-respect in ways I had never imagined growing up. "If the bullies could only see me now," I thought.

The younger players, sophomores, looked up to me as much or more… no, definitely more than my peers did. They were much more impressed with the fact that I was born without a left hand, had played baseball and was now about to become a fullback on the varsity football team! My senior and junior teammates just saw me as "Lynn." They kept me grounded and I didn't let this stuff go to my head (too much). After all, I didn't start on the JV team and wasn't a super star. I was just part of a very good team.

Two-a-days were the same as always, but different -- Maturing bodies that have been through the drills and routines so many times before react quicker and do things with more finesse. We were once boys, but now felt like men. We did the drills with more snap. We got off the ball more crisply. We ran faster, harder and with more gusto. We blocked better, tackled better and knew the game much better. Our defensive backs could cover receivers better than they ever had. Our receivers were more sure-handed now and ran more exacting routes. All the players from JV had gotten more experienced and more confident in their individual abilities as well as those of the team.

But with all that said; only two of us were returning varsity lettermen, Randy Rossi and Scott McKenzie; great players, indeed, but the rest of us were untried under fire in a varsity game. The crowds would be bigger... much bigger. Our opponents would be more talented than anyone we had previously faced. And we had the added pressure of being expected to live up to the winning tradition of so many Long Beach Woodrow Wilson Champions of the past despite being picked by the sports writers to likely finish in fourth place in the Moore League.

With training camp now behind us the varsity depth chart was revealed and I immediately saw that I had made the team, although I was listed as the number three fullback at that point. Conflicted by the excitement of making the team but placed behind Larry Newbill and a junior, Rex Hoover, who was listed as the first-string fullback,

A Cinderella Team...Time to Be Bold

motivated me even more to prove to the coaches that their choice of starting fullback was a mistake (at least as far as I was concerned).

As with the previous years, the Milk Bowl was to be the debut of our varsity team. I would be playing in one of the quarter-long contests played between us and Jordan High School. I was excited about that opportunity, except for one problem; I had injured my lower back muscles in practice a week before. It was so painful I had to roll myself out of bed in order to be able to stand up. I went to our official team doctor's office and had multiple ultra-sound treatments that helped, but I wasn't 100 percent or even 80% on the day of the Milk Bowl. I couldn't even touch my fingers to the ground when we were supposed to be in our three-point stances, let alone my knuckles (this turned out to be a blessing in disguise in the future because I learned that if I just touched my fingertips to the ground instead of my knuckles I could get a quicker start off the ball). But I was determined to play and didn't let on to the coaches just how much pain I was in.

Since I would be playing only one period and both teams would no doubt have the ball at least once, I believed I could hang in there for the 12-minute "game." In front of a typical full-house Milk Bowl crowd at Long Beach Veterans Stadium, both of our squads offensively and defensively played fairly well. The one mistake I made that probably did more to hurt my chances of playing more rather than less at the beginning of the season was not recognizing that in the formation we were in the hole created by our linemen's blocks that I was supposed to carry the ball through would be wider than when we were in the T-formation.

When the ball was snapped I ran too far to the inside and got stacked up just beyond the line of scrimmage. Had I ran where I was supposed to, as the game films later clearly showed, I might have gained twenty yards or even scored. Instead, we had to punt. Coach Dixon barked, "You could've driven a truck through that hole," as I came to the sideline. I was mortified. "How many chances to prove yourself do you think you're going to get, dummy," I thought to myself. Not an auspicious debut on the varsity.

Costly mistakes and a lack of varsity experience were the biggest factors in our lackluster performance during the non-conference, preseason games we played. The high note was our gradual improvement over the course of these four games and our exceptional team spirit. Non-conference games typically gave the coaches an opportunity to judge the overall talent of their team and a chance, generally, to play as many players as makes sense to help them gain playing time and build their confidence. It would have been great had they actually done that in my case.

Although I was performing well in our practices, I didn't get into any of these non-conference games. It would be so much more gratifying to write here that I emerged as a star and that I played quite a bit, but that is not what happened. It was monumentally frustrating to me because I believed deep down to my very core that I should have been the starting fullback. Most players who aren't starters feel this way, of course, but for me this was torture.

Our coaches were accustomed to winning and usually winning big. We were a challenge for them and their coaching skills. Coach Rowland, who had been the head coach for many years, stepped aside to allow Coach Dixon to take on that role purportedly so Skip wouldn't have to deal with the sports writers, who he mostly didn't care for. Over the years he had coached some excellent players and he was a good judge of talent. But I was convinced that because Rex Hoover was six-foot, one-inches tall, a bit faster than me and was a junior, which meant he would be a formidable running back the following year, Rowland had made him the starter. I am not certain, but I suspected that Skip also wasn't too excited about playing his one-handed senior fullback in important games. Had we been winning, and the scores lopsided in our favor, perhaps I would have played in these non-conference games, but we lost to Western High School 10-7, Warren High School 28-14, and to perennial power house, Mater Dei by a score of 20-0. The only non-conference game we won was against Alhambra High School, by a score of 21-14.

After our second game I was walking from our locker room when Coach Dixon drove his car up beside me and rolled down his window. He then asked me to learn to play defensive end in practice the next week. He thought I would have a better opportunity to play defense than trying to be a running back (the implication here was that I wasn't playing because the risk of my fumbling was too high to chance it). If I had wanted to just watch the games I could have bought a ticket. Since I wanted to play and hadn't as yet, I agreed to give it a shot, all the while giving my best effort when I practiced at fullback. It was clear to me that Coach Dixon wanted me to be playing... somewhere.

I had studied the defensive-end responsibilities well over the weekend. On the first day in practice on defense I was paying close attention to everything Coach Dixon was saying. At one point he was trying to show the defensive ends a particular movement and positioning when there was an offensive pulling-guard coming your way and how to take him on in order to disrupt the running play and possibly make the tackle. The first two guys got it wrong, more than once. On my first try I nailed it. Coach Dixon immediately said, "Why can't you guys get this? Effinger got it right the first time and you've been practicing for weeks!" I scored points with Coach Dixon the first day. Good sign.

During our next game at Warren High School in Buena Park, things weren't going well. At halftime the line coach, Mr. Morton, was grousing so I piped up saying that he should put me in the game because I wouldn't be screwing up like the player who was at defensive end in the first half. Not a wise move. Coaches want teammates to be supportive, not be someone seeking to tear at someone else to benefit personally. My frustration at not even getting a *chance* to play got the better of me. Coach let me know he wasn't pleased and I never spouted off again... publicly.

It appeared to most observers that the sports writers had called it right - the Wilson varsity was headed for a fourth-place finish in the Moore League. But events unfolded during the Mater Dei game that changed our course. Down 20-0 after two quarters, during halftime the situation seemed hopeless and admittedly the whole team looked defeated. Just then, Coach Dixon, who had a streak of Vince Lombardi in him, grabbed one of our biggest players and tossed him into the door of a locker. His face was as red as our helmets. He started berating us and said, "You guys are a disgrace to the honor of Wilson High football, and you should be ashamed of yourselves!"

He didn't stop there. He singled out some of the mistakes players had made and said we were gutless and conceding to Mater Dei based on their reputation, not their actual ability. He said he was embarrassed of our performance and that we had better decide right then and there whether or not we should stay on the team. It was classic! Apparently it was exactly what was needed, as the team went out and kept Mater Dei scoreless in the second half. Although we didn't score either it was obvious that our defense could stop even the best teams from scoring many points if they gave it all they had.

At practice on Monday as we began to prepare for our first conference opponent, Millikan High School, instead of haranguing us for the loss, the coaches praised the team for showing their mettle in the face of tough odds. They now knew what they had and how to coach us to victory moving forward. They noted that we had shown steady improvement and a team spirit that was higher than previous varsity teams at Wilson. Dixon stressed that we must make up for any deficiencies in pure talent with teamwork. No one was better than any other player. We would win as a team or lose as a team, but we were going to play as a team, no matter what.

I had an excellent week of practice on both offense and defense and was hopeful, yet not confident, that I would play this week. We opened league competition by jolting Millikan, 13-7. Both teams exchanged unsuccessful scoring drives in the first half, but our quarterback, Dick Burdge spearheaded a 13-point third quarter. He drove the offense 66 yards down the field and capped it off with a one-yard dive into the end zone. The extra-point try failed and it was now Wilson six and Millikan zero.

After Millikan failed to move when they got the ball we again drove deep into their territory where a fake field goal attempt surprised their defense. With Millikan anticipating another score, second-team quarterback Gary Carter tossed a 7-yard TD pass to Chris Key. Jeff Burroughs' extra point was good and we were up 13-0. Although Millikan later scored once, our defense limited the Rams to a total of just three first downs and we won the game. Our defensive standouts that glorious night were Randy Rossi, Scott McKenzie, Bob Graves, Mark Lewis and Wes Edwards. We had stunned our first league opponent. I was amazed, and disappointed, that I didn't get to play again, but winning tempered my frustration... a little.

Another great week of practice preceded our next game against Downey High School at home. Practices had by this time become my games. I practiced as if I were playing in a real game. It helped me cope with not playing in the real games. If I was practicing as hard as I could, I knew I was helping the team as best I could under the circumstances. After the hard-fought victory at Millikan, we made it two wins in a row by dismantling Downey 46-0. Our offense had a field day with touchdowns contributed

A Cinderella Team...Time to Be Bold

by Rex Hoover, Dante Lobato, Mike Leininger, Randy Rossi and Lynn Effinger. Lynn Effinger? Yep, I finally saw action.

We were up by a couple of touchdowns and suddenly, unexpectedly, I actually heard Coach Rowland yell my name! I ran over to him and he rattled off the play he wanted me to take in. It was a running play... to the fullback. I relayed the play to Dick Burdge and we lined up. Dick called signals. We got into our three-point stance and when Dick yelled, "Hut," we snapped into action. I took the handoff and an arm flew at me and hit the ball popping it up a bit as I broke through the line. I immediately got control of the ball and gained about six yards. I jumped up and sprinted back to the huddle, my adrenalin on high from the excitement of finally getting to play. As that ball had popped up I could clearly hear Coach Rowland yelling from the sideline, "Protect the ball." Not figuratively; I could actually hear him yelling at me. Do you think he was nervous with me out there?

Although our offense was somehow held to only six points in the first quarter, on the first two drives in the second quarter we scored two touchdowns. Dante Lobato scored twice on running plays, one of which was a result of pure speed on Dante's part. Jeff Burroughs then hit Mike Leininger for a 37-yard touchdown pass. As later reported in our yearbook, "Lynn Effinger, after darting through the Downey defenders, also scored." After scoring my first varsity touchdown I threw the ball high into the night sky and ran over and jumped up on Mark Lewis. He was as happy as I was. What a feeling! It's hard to describe the rush one gets from scoring a varsity touchdown.

For me, it was one of the greatest feelings I had ever experienced up to that moment; much like hitting a home run. Again, from our yearbook, "Offensive standouts included Dick Burdge, Jeff Burroughs, Lynn Effinger, and Ferando Trinidade who kicked three extra-point conversions." That was more like it!

We out-performed the Downey squad in every category accumulating 393 yards of total offense against their 142. We had 18 first downs, Downey had two. Our defense recovered a fumble and made three interceptions. It was a big night and I had played a role in our victory! I was on cloud nine, or was it ten? I had fought hard to make this team, practiced extra diligently to earn a chance to play, had been mightily disappointed because I hadn't yet played and now, it all became worth the effort and frustration. I received accolades from students, teachers, my coaches and my parents. This is what I had dreamed of and prepared for these past three years. I got a boost to my self-esteem that was immeasurable.

On the following Monday after practice we watched game films as usual. When the film reached the first offensive plays where I was in the game, it showed me jumping up after each play and running, not walking or jogging back to the huddle. Coach Dixon commented, "Here's one of the things I like about Lynn, he has a burning desire to play and you can tell that by his actions, not words." Amen.

The rivalry between Long Beach Polytechnic High School and Woodrow Wilson High School dated back decades before our senior year. It was (and still is) one of the biggest cross-town rivalries in California. The football games between these two schools were almost always close, hard-fought contests between some of the best high school football players in the country, let alone in California and in Long Beach. The 1967 game was no different.

The 36th annual "Big Game" resulted in a surprising upset win for our team, one of the most important of the year. Before a rambunctious sell-out crowd of approximately 15,000 people at Veterans Stadium, early on in the first period Rex Hoover jolted over the goal line from the two-yard line, giving us a 6-0 lead. Poly led by 7-6 at the start of the third quarter, but cornerback Gary Carter led our defense on two game-deciding plays. Early in the fourth quarter as Poly received a punt, Gary capitalized on a costly Jackrabbit fumble on the Poly four-yard line. As the loose football flipped into the end zone, Gary recovered it and scored. In the final minutes of the contest he made a crucial stop on a Poly first down attempt, denying Poly a scoring opportunity. Other defensive highlights were contributed by Wes Edwards, Larry Newbill, Scott McKenzie, Mark Lewis and Randy Rossi (do you see a pattern here?). The offense also shined as Dick Burdge teamed up with Chris Key, Rex Hoover, Pat Mathews and Dante Lobato on time-consuming drives.

This was as important a victory as we would ever have. Our team came into the game a serious underdog, performed at its peak, made big plays when we had to and snatched victory from the jaws of defeat. When that Jackrabbit player tried to field the punt inside the ten-yard line, which is almost never attempted at any level in football and Gary Carter recovered it for a score, we started seriously believing that we were destined to be Moore League Champions.

The statistics for the game clearly show that it was a defensive battle and how close this game was:

	Wilson	Poly
Total First Downs	12	10
Total Yards Rushing	175	201
Total Yards Passing	33	32
Total Yards Gained	213	233
Penalties/Yards	4/30	4/20

I'm sure you noticed that my name is conspicuously absent among the standouts. It is what it is, but I was sure excited to be on the winning team that night. Rex Hoover had struggled a little bit to gain yardage during the game and I thought I'd get in, but it was not to be. Before the game, Coach Dixon had told me he expected me to play that night, so I was pumped up. My name was never called. Instead, I supported my teammates as best I could from the sideline.

We moved into first place the following week by defeating Jordan High School 34-0. Millikan had handed Lakewood its first loss of the season, and we had beat Millikan the week before. We were in the driver's seat, at the moment. We were now the leading contender for the Moore League Title. Chants of, "We're Number One," permeated the night air as we pummeled the Jordan Panthers. Our ground game, always our mainstay, dominated the contest. Dante had 164 yards by *himself*. According to the account of the game in our yearbook, "Touchdowns included tallies by Lobato, Hoover, Lynn Effinger, and Chris Key."

I played well in this game and contributed to our victory in no small measure, as Rex had another off night. I remember watching him make several tries to eventually score down inside the six-yard line, thinking to myself that I would have pounded in there on the first attempt. But we'll never know, of course, and I could have been wrong. But when I did get a shot I scored on my first attempt from the five. Again, I was so excited I threw that ball about 35 yards through the back of the end zone, a clear penalty these days, but nobody said a word to me. Did I ever tell you how exhilarating it is to score a varsity touchdown? I was then moved up to second string on the depth chart. Progress sometimes comes slowly. While it is often difficult, patience can be a virtue. So too can boldness.

Our final regular season game against heavily favored Lakewood High School was going to define who we were as a Wilson High School Football Team. Together, as a tight-knit group of enthusiastic, hard-working guys whose chances of winning a championship had been all but written off by pundits, we had struggled mightily in the pre-season before snapping out of our malaise to hold Mater Dei scoreless in the second half of that game and began a string of conference victories. We were now on the precipice. With a win or even a tie with Lakewood we would be Moore League Champions and demonstrate that we had what it takes to play and win for Woodrow Wilson

High School. If we lost we would end up in third place; Big difference.

We had an outstanding week of practice leading up to the game on Friday night. Everyone was confident we had a shot at the title despite being a serious underdog to the 7-1 Lancers, 3-1 in conference play. We were 5-3 for the year and 4-0 in league play. The coaches had put up signs all over the locker room saying, "Omaha... No Prisoners!" to pump us up. Coach Dixon was an Army World War II veteran who was among those brave young men on D-Day in June of 1944 who stormed the beaches of Normandy. He was with them on deadly Omaha Beach. He wanted us to take this game seriously and have a mind-set that focused on performing at our highest possible level. So much so that he brought a couple of WWII veterans who participated in the D-Day invasion to address the team. They stressed that each individual on that beach had done their part to support each other and found a way to persevere. Coach Dixon told us that we needed to be bold, brave and as determined as ever to come out victorious. I know these marshal references "offend" some people, but it matters not to me. This was going to be a battle; one winner; one loser. This was war.

The Championship Game was a big game; too big to be played on either high school's football field. So, again we were going to play at Veterans Stadium. The attendance that night was estimated to be over 17,000 students, relatives and fans. It seemed as if I could hear every single one of them from inside our locker room. Under the stadium we could hear the vibrant sounds of our drummers and the other instruments of our marching band. The sound echoed through the room pumping us up before the game to heights we had never before experienced. There was tension in that locker room; more because of anticipation than hesitation. We had practiced and practiced for this game all year long. We had traveled the long road of struggle, defeat and redemption together as a team. A team that had proven its mettle in the many days and weeks that had passed was now emboldened to believe, in ourselves, in our abilities, and in what we saw as our destiny. We believed we would achieve… together.

We said a team prayer and marched out towards the field. I was the first player out of the locker room and the first to run through the huge paper banner stretched across the field between the cheerleaders. We were all screaming, "Omaha!" This was the night for which I had prepared myself and I was determined to be a part of Wilson history, to contribute to our collective efforts. With a championship and playoff berth on the line, we were about to get it on.

As was always the case, I didn't start the game… but I was sent in several times in the first half to replace Rex on offense and Larry on defense. I was in the game on offense when the first half ended. We were down 20-7 at the half, disappointed but not dejected. It was mostly quiet in the locker room as the coaches instructed us as to what adjustments we needed to make to gain the upper hand. Coach Dixon then gave us a rousing halftime pep talk and told us that this was it. We had to go back out there and play our guts out and have the best half of any game we ever played.

"Don't give up, and don't give in... Omaha!" he yelled.

"Omaha!" we all echoed back in unison at the top of our lungs.

Our coaches had always instructed us that if we were in the game at the end of a quarter, whether we had started the game or not, we were to stay in until replaced by the coaches. Just before the end of the first half I was in and Rex was not. We received the second-half kickoff. As our offensive team took the field Rex started toward the huddle. I ran over to him and told him, firmly, that he was out and I was in. He had a confused look on his face but went directly back to the sidelines. Now, I didn't really think the coaches considered halftime to be treated the same as any other quarter, but it made no difference to me. I was a senior. I had worked my butt off to play varsity football, not watch it. This was the final regular-season game of my high school football career, possibly the last game that I would ever play. I had followed (or rather tweaked) Coach Dixon's advice at a critical time, believing that in this case I'd seek forgiveness, rather than permission. I was being bold, perhaps as bold as I'd ever been.

I was in on every offensive play of the second half. I didn't hear Coach Rowland say this because I was in the middle of the field at the time playing football, but Jim Creighton, one of my best buddies heard Rowland loudly ask no one in particular, "What's Effinger doing in there?" According to Jim, Coach Dixon then yelled back, "Leave

A Cinderella Team...Time to Be Bold

him in there!" I remained in the game for the duration. I played well; ran hard with the ball, blocked my tail off and felt a bigger part of the team than I ever, ever had before. My longest run was 14 yards and would have been longer but I chose to run over, rather than around the defender that ran up to me from the left. I've wanted to smack those on the left ever since. It took three Lancer defenders to bring me down.

On one play I was handed the ball and went off left tackle. I was hit hard just two yards from the line of scrimmage. As I was getting up out of the pile I heard one of Lakewood's defensive lineman say, "Run this way again and I'll tear your other arm off!"

Whoa!! I was beyond ticked now! In the huddle I told Dick to give me the ball. He told me, rightfully so, to shut up. Then he called my number again. Same play, same hole. Jim Hunt, our big, strong offensive tackle said, "Follow me Lynn, we'll kick his ass." And we did. I ran over this jerk for nearly a five-yard gain.

Late in the fourth quarter, reserve quarterback, Gary Carter connected on a 15-yard touchdown pass to split-end, Chris Key. We were behind by seven points. With less than two minutes remaining in the game while I was still out on the field, we were just about to score again when we were stopped by a Lakewood interception on the Lancer three. The Lakewood side of the stadium erupted into the loudest cheer of the night. There had been many of them throughout the game. Our side of the stadium was stricken with deafening silence. During a time out, Coach Dixon grabbed Wes Edwards by the facemask and snarled at him to go out and kick all of our defensive linemen in the butt and tell them to go after the football. Returning to the field Wes did as he was instructed. Lakewood seemed to have the game locked up... until a miracle happened; a fired up Bruin defensive charge led by Scott McKenzie caused a fumble in the end zone and Larry Newbill immediately fell on the ball, clutching it for dear life. He had scored a touchdown!

Now we were down 20-19 with just over one minute to go in the game. All we needed was a successful extra-point try and we would tie the game and win the Moore League Championship! The field-goal kicking team, of which I was part, ran onto the field. Our normal kicker was, Ferando Trinidade, who was a South American exchange student who kicked soccer style (rare in high school back then). He had, of course, never played American football before coming to the United States. He was able to kick the ball farther than our other kickers, but often with less accuracy and sometimes too low.

Meaning no offense to Ferando here, the coaches wisely sent in Jeff Burroughs, the future first-round draft pick of the Texas Rangers, to attempt the point after. I will never forget the look on Jeff's face when he came into the huddle — his eyes were bugged out and his face looked more pale than usual. But Jeff was a tremendous competitor. He would be Wilson's starting quarterback the following season. He had a good leg and abundant confidence in himself. The signals were called, the ball was snapped right to our holder, Gary Carter, then Jeff moved forward and began his kicking motion... the crowd was hushed for the first time all night. As the ball left Jeff's foot I hit the outside defender as hard as I could and then looked up. The ball sailed right between the uprights. The referee signaled that it was good! We did it! A dramatic 20-20 tie to give us the Championship! The Wilson side of the stadium exploded into a rousing, sustained cheer that surely could be heard for miles around. The silence that engulfed the Lancer's fans was resoundingly revealing. Just as we had done on the junior varsity the previous year, we tied Lakewood in our final game of the season but won the league championship!

Moments later after the gun went off signaling the end of this magnificent game, as was tradition, the team, students and alumni from Wilson sang our alma mater, *Hail to Wilson*. It never sounded so sweet! We were battered, bruised, sore, tired, proud and overjoyed all at once. This truly was a "Cinderella Season" as the newspapers would say the following morning.

Most of the rest of that night remains a blur, but it was one of the most rewarding, fulfilling experiences of my life and one in which I am so proud to have played a considerable role. Had I not been bold and assertive, sending Rex Hoover to the sidelines on my own it could have been a whole different story, at least for me. I learned a valuable lesson that night, in addition to all the others I had learned over the years: Don't let anything or anyone stand in your way of achieving your goals if it is at all possible; Leave nothing to chance, be bold, take the initiative, and most importantly, persevere.

Believe to Achieve

1967 Wilson High School Varsity Football Team (I am number 32 in the front row between Mark Lewis and Jeff Burroughs.

At our 40th High School Reunion at the Long Beach Yacht Club in 2008 I got to see many of my senior teammates again, which was a great thrill. Wes Edwards, my friend who always treated me with kindness and respect dating back to the fifth grade, somehow, somewhere came across a DVD recording that had been transferred from the original 16-mm film of the Lakewood game. He showed it all night at the reunion on a laptop. You know how guys are always saying how good they were back in the day when maybe they've embellished it to pump themselves up in the eyes of others? Well, this DVD speaks for itself. I now have a copy of it and the truth is that I played better in that game than I remembered. Showing it to my kids and grandchildren was another highlight of my blessed life.

By winning the Moore League title our team qualified for the CIF Championship tournament. It is a typical single-elimination tournament with the champions of one league playing the champions of another until there is one team left standing from the Northern and Southern Sections of the CIF who play each other for the state championship. It is an honor to play in the CIF Championship series.

We had the misfortune of being slated to play Anaheim High School in the first round of the playoffs. Anaheim had destroyed everyone they played and was heavily favored to win our game. The sports writers predicted that they would ultimately be crowned CIF Champions. They were jam-packed with incredibly talented, big players, including their High School All-Everything fullback, Tom Fitzpatrick, one of the best in the country, who was later recruited by the University of Southern California.

During practice that week the atmosphere was uncommonly relaxed. We were still on a high from the Lakewood game and although we were excited to be in the CIF playoffs, we knew that this time we might well be seen as the underdog for good reason. We were determined to do our best to represent the Moore League, however, and Wilson tradition. On Monday the coaches handed out the little signs with "Omaha" written on them that had been all over our locker room the week before to the players they felt had been standouts against Lakewood. I still have mine that was inscribed by Coach Rowland, which says, "Thanks Lynn for undying loyalty and spirit." Another note from Coach Rowland said, "Lynn, Tremendous Season!"

You want recognition, Lynn? How about validation? Here you go. I was jubilant, as you can surely imagine. Getting that kind of praise right out in front of my teammates was as good as it gets. I'll never forget it for as long as I live.

The CIF playoff game itself, again played before a huge crowd at Veterans Stadium, was certainly a disappointment. We lost 35-13. I played most of the game, my last in high school and did well once again. On an interception that our quarterback threw late in the game I ran down the player who had intercepted the pass and clobbered him on the sideline, head first, driving him out of bounds. I got back what I gave as I was momentarily knocked out cold. As the final gun went off signaling the end of the game, the end of our playoff hopes and the end of our senior season, I started walking to the bus. Only I walked the wrong way. Coach Rowland had to come get me and direct me in the right direction. I wasn't seeing butterflies, but I was still a bit dinged, apparently. Our loss to Anaheim was made a bit more acceptable when they won the state CIF Championship, handily. They were truly a great team and it was gratifying that if we had to lose we lost to the best team in our state.

A Cinderella Team...Time to Be Bold

To this day people at Wilson High School and around Long Beach talk about our winning the title and our incredible, inexplicable Cinderella Season... and our team. It would be many years before another Wilson varsity football team won a Moore League Championship. To be a part of something as special as the 1967 football season is hard to describe and understand. And to fulfill my personal goal in such a dramatic fashion is nothing short of miraculous and I'm not being hyperbolic here. I believe in divine providence.

There is no such thing as luck except that which you create yourself, individually as well as collectively. Luck is what happens when preparedness meets opportunity. I was born at the right time in the right place. I ultimately became a part of something so special and wonderful that it is hard not to believe that God intended for all of this to happen just as it did. I was born without a left hand for a reason, as well. And I am honestly, deeply and earnestly grateful to God for that. The real "reason" I was born this way, and the only reason that matters, was about to be revealed to me soon after this remarkable chapter of my life.

Chapter Eight

—

My "Responsibility"

"You never know when a moment and a few sincere words can have an impact on a life."

– Zig Ziglar

My "Responsibility"

ON THE DAY OF OUR football awards dinner in early January of 1968 Coach Dixon asked me if my parents were both coming to the dinner. I said I thought so, but wasn't certain. He barked at me once again, saying, "Well, they both better be."

That seemed a bit odd, but the thought crossed my mind that maybe, just maybe I was getting an award in addition to my Varsity Letter? Nah, there must be another explanation. But, I thought, maybe I'll be named Most Inspirational Player, which would be quite an honor? I didn't really think so, however.

That night, with Mom and Dad sitting beside me, I watched and listened intently as Wes Edwards was named Most Valuable Player of the Year, Scott McKenzie was named Defensive Lineman of the Year and Jim Hunt was named Offensive Lineman of the Year. Dante Lobato was named Back of the Year, and the Most Inspirational Player award went to... Dick Burdge. I was happy for Dick, because he had been inspirational and deserved special recognition for his contribution to our winning the championship. Under different circumstances he would have most likely earned Back of the Year honors, but Dante, a junior, really had a standout season. I sadly admit to being a bit disappointed, but hey, I wasn't a star or even a starter, so I accepted it.

Then Coach Dixon started talking about a new annual award that the coaches had created. He described the qualities a player would have to have in order to receive such an award; Desire, determination, fierce competitiveness, loyalty to the team and coaches and to Woodrow Wilson

High School. Most importantly, Dixon said, the player who would be given this special award each year had to have heart. Then he brought up the team doctor to present the award, saying, "This year we are honored to present the First Annual Courage Award to... Lynn Effinger."

My jaw almost hit the floor. Amidst loud applause I walked to the front of the room, looking at all the smiling faces of my teammates and their parents. It was an overwhelmingly emotional moment. I forced myself not to lose it in front of these young men. Coach Dixon said some very complimentary things about me and thanked me for my contribution to the team, handing me my beautiful trophy. Upon returning to my seat my mother gave me big hug and Dad shook my hand. I could see tears in their eyes once again and could tell how proud they were of me at that moment; recognition and validation.

For the record, I did not feel the least bit courageous. To my mind I had simply set a very important personal goal to play varsity football by the time I was a senior. I had a burning desire to achieve that goal, worked hard to accomplish it, was determined to succeed, was bold and gave it my very best each and every step of the way. But I was sure proud to receive that award and hoped it wouldn't be the last time I was rewarded for my performance.

On the way home from the awards dinner, Dad let me drive Mom's car. My girlfriend at the time, Roslyn Bixby (one of the few I really ever had), was babysitting my younger brother and sister for my parents at our house so they could attend the awards dinner. I was so excited to be going home to show Roz the trophy I had received that my foot was a little heavy to the metal. Sure enough, a

My "Responsibility"

motorcycle cop pulled me over. Dad wasn't too happy, but under the circumstances he didn't say a word. When the officer asked me to show him my driver's license I realized that I hadn't brought it with me from home. Oops! The police officer asked me if I had any other form of identification. I said, no, but then I added, "I have a trophy that I got tonight that has my name on it." I showed it to him; he looked at it, and only gave me a warning instead of a ticket. Perhaps "courage" was a good thing to possess. It certainly was fortuitous.

A couple of weeks later I was invited to attend the Twelfth Annual Long Beach Century Club Sports Night Awards Banquet to be held on January 25, 1968 (my mother's 39th birthday). It was to be held in downtown Long Beach at the renowned Lafayette Hotel. This was a very special annual event that was attended by local business men and women, city dignitaries and special guests from the sporting world. High school, college and other local athletes were recognized annually by the Century Club for their outstanding achievements in sports the preceding year. Earl McCullough, the former football star at Long Beach Poly High School and the University of Southern California, who would later play in the NFL for the Detroit Lions, was going to be honored as Athlete of the Year. Interestingly, in hindsight, one of the sports personalities attending the awards dinner that evening was O.J. Simpson from USC. Other guests included Billie Jean King, Head Coach George Allen of the Los Angeles Rams, John McKay, Head Coach for USC and other notables of that era.

I had no idea why I had been invited. There were only three high school football players from Long Beach schools invited to attend this gala, and one of them was me. It was an honor to be invited for whatever reason. My parents also attended.

Wes Edwards, my friend and teammate at Wilson was being named high school Defensive Player of the Year. Mike Liebeck, an excellent halfback from Millikan was the Offensive Player of the Year. Unbelievably, I was being honored as the "Most Courageous Football Player of the Decade." There was that word again, "courageous." I was honored in the extreme to receive such recognition but again, I did not feel that I was particularly courageous. I felt that courage was something that our troops in Vietnam possessed, but not me. Admittedly, this truly was a remarkable conclusion to my quest to play varsity football at Wilson High School. I never dreamed of receiving such high recognition.

In my senior yearbook, Coach Dixon wrote:

"To a fine football player. I'm sure you never expected what happened to you this year. You deserve everything & more. What a contribution you have made to Wilson. Congratulations, Coach Dixon."

Late in the spring of my senior year while I was in my English my class a student came in and handed my teacher a slip of paper. She called me up to her desk and handed me the note. It was from Coach Crutchfield. It was a request from him to come to his office right away. I had no idea why I had been summoned to see him, so I thought about what I could possibly have done wrong…

My "Responsibility"

that he would know about anyway, that might have been the catalyst for such a meeting. Nothing came to mind, so I figured I might as well leave my class and go to see him as requested. I always did as Mr. Crutchfield requested. As stated earlier, he had been a huge part of my achieving my goals relative to playing varsity football.

When I arrived and entered Coach Crutchfield's cramped office there was a student sitting in a chair next to Coach's always tidy desk. I noticed that the student had an arm that was missing fingers on one of his hands that was similar to mine. Mr. Crutchfield asked me to tell this young man about some of my athletic achievements and the positive recognition and enhanced self-esteem I had received as a result. The young man also had the look on his face of someone who actually had done something wrong and Coach had called him on it. I'll be honest here and say that in no way, shape or form did I consider myself to be any kind of role model.

I spoke to the kid as Coach had instructed me. I'm not sure my comments had the desired positive impact on this student in the long run, but he did seem to respond in a positive way that afternoon. I was relieved when I had finished my unsolicited assignment. Mr. Crutchfield was pleased, which in turn pleased me. But then he jolted me by what he said next. Coach leaned forward, with his face close to mine, put his strong right hand on my shoulder and said to me in a very serious tone, "Lynn, you have a responsibility."

I thought to myself, "Great, I'm 17 years old and don't really want the responsibilities I already have, so why is Coach saying this to me and what can he possibly mean?"

He continued, "Because of the success you have had playing baseball and football despite your birth defect, you have a responsibility to help teach others how to overcome adversity to be the best they can be."

I listened closely to what he said, but I had no clue as to how I was supposed to live up to such a duty. I returned to my class still thinking about what Coach Crutchfield said, but I really didn't know how in the world I would go about helping others in that way. Instead of dwelling on it, I decided to concentrate on what was going on in my classes. I was going to be graduating in June and had to start thinking about what my major would be in college and whether or not I was going to go out for the football team at Long Beach City College, where I expected to attend in the fall. It would be a lot tougher to make a college team, I knew, even if it was a junior college. Long Beach City College was one of the biggest and best in California. Their football teams had always been successful. After all, they drew players from Wilson, Poly, Lakewood, Millikan, Jordan, and St. Anthony's high schools.

Graduation was held across the street from Wilson High at Blair Field, a small major-league sized baseball stadium where our varsity baseball team played their biggest rivals because of the seating capacity. The Chicago Cubs had held Spring Training there my sophomore year and the Los Angeles Rams of the NFL were now using it during football season as a training facility and a practice field. I saw Willie Mays hit a home run over the center field fence against the Cubs, and it was great watching the Rams players arrive and leave each day. Sometimes we could coerce them into giving us autographs.

My "Responsibility"

The Graduation ceremonies were nice, but the awareness that adulthood, with all the attendant responsibilities and challenges it would bring, was staring me in the face. It was a bit intimidating, mostly because I wasn't sure what I wanted to do for the rest of my life. I had no idea that things would evolve as they eventually did. I probably wouldn't have believed it if someone could have told me about it beforehand.

The year of my graduation, 1968, is said by many historians to be one of the most significant, tumultuous years in history. It was that and much more. In 2008 *Time* magazine devoted an entire issue to the subject. During that single year we witnessed the Tet Offensive and the First Battle of Saigon in South Vietnam which shocked the American media and begat calls for our troops to be withdrawn. The My Lai Massacre took place, which the American people would not find out about until November of 1969. Martin Luther King, Jr. had been gunned down in Memphis on April 4th by James Earl Ray. Bobby Kennedy was on the campaign trail following his victory in the California presidential primary election. He was assassinated at the Ambassador Hotel in Los Angeles. He was killed by an angry, militant Muslim man named Sirhan Sirhan. Angry, militant Muslims would, of course, grow in numbers and do harm to America, Americans and others for decades to follow. Nearly 4,000 Soviet tanks invaded Czechoslovakia. Police clashed with ant-war protestors in Chicago, Illinois outside the Democratic National Convention. This did not portend well for young people leaving the security and comfort of high school to enter the real world and become adults.

That following summer our coaches had come up with a perpetual trophy, or rather a large plaque that would annually list the senior football players' names who had been named Defensive Player of the Year, Offensive Player of the Year, Most Valuable Player of the Year and Most Inspirational Player of the Year. This was different than the awards given at our varsity banquet, because Dante Lobato, a junior, had been named Offensive Player of the Year and Dick Burdge had been named Most Inspirational Player of the Year. On this inaugural plaque the honorees were, Scott McKenzie, Dick Burdge, Wes Edwards, and me, respectively. This meant that I had achieved recognition as Most Inspirational *Senior* Player; another incredible honor.

My parents never really stressed to my brothers and sister and I the importance of getting a college education. Dad certainly had made no plans to finance our attending a major college or university. It wasn't a priority in either my dad's or my mom's families and none of Dad's uncles or aunts ever went to college, nor did Mom's as far as I know. Dad had dropped out of high school in Detroit, earning his GED in the Navy. He was mostly a self-educated man

My "Responsibility"

who was a voracious reader and student of real life. He was a hard-working, intelligent, resourceful and creative individual who wasn't afraid to take calculated risks and overcome challenges to achieve success. He had achieved a good deal of success without having a college degree. We were expected to do well in school and get good grades, of course, but there was no expectation that we would go to college, much less earn a degree of any kind.

I was somewhat ambivalent about going to college, which in hindsight I should not have been. So many of my fellow high school graduates were going to attend USC, UCLA, Stanford, Long Beach State College and other schools including Long Beach City College that I thought I should at least consider going to LBCC. Dad wasn't going to pay for me to go to college unless it was to LBCC, so if I was going to go to college anywhere it would be there. Besides, although I had worked for my father as a laborer on his construction sites, worked at a car wash, and as a busboy at Hof's Hut in Belmont Shore while in high school, I had no clue as to what line of work I was going to pursue. Going to college, even a community college, seemed like a good place to figure that out.

Chapter Nine

College, Marriage, and More

"Happy marriages begin when we marry the ones we love, and they blossom when we love the ones we marry."

– Tom Mullen

College, Marriage, and More

I HAD MET WITH THE head football coach at LBCC prior to graduating from high school. At that time he said he knew all about me, was impressed and he hoped I would consider playing for him next season. He said he wanted me to weigh more than 190 pounds when training camp started. As summer progressed I thought a lot about going to LBCC and wondered if I should play football. I finally decided I would enroll and go out for the team. Dennis Dummit, Denny Mayfield, Jeff Severson and a couple of the others who played varsity for Wilson in 1966 were now stars for the Vikings. They encouraged me to play. There were only a few of us from the 1967 Bruin team who planned to play football at LBCC; Chris Key, Jim Hunt, Tom Crowell, Gary Carter, Mark Lewis and me. After making the decision to play I worked out in the Long Beach *State* College weight room every day after school, because the athletic director allowed me to, even though I was still in high school. I also ran pass patterns with other players from Long Beach State and LBCC whenever they were around. I also worked out there during the summer. But there was no driving force at this point to compel me to accomplish much more than to make the team and have an opportunity to play college football, which not many people had ever thought possible.

On the first day of summer training camp for the 1968 season at LBCC there had to be 120 or 130 guys who came to tryouts from all the local high schools. The varsity team could only carry half that many or probably less when the regular season began. We were told coming in to expect some very intense practice sessions. Early on they would consist of a lot of drills and running, and more running. This was one way for the coaches to separate the men from the boys and as guys didn't show up for the next practice because of all the running and intense drills it made it easier to pare down the number of guys that would make the team prior to the coaches' actual cuts.

Drill after drill after drill, all morning, followed by laps around the field. At the end of each practice we did 40-yard wind sprints, unless the coaches wanted us to run the "down-set-go drill." Our receivers coach (I can't recall his name, but he was a backup wide receiver for a couple of years behind Raymond Berry for the Baltimore Colts), loved to have us run this drill. By position, you get up to the goal line and line up horizontally across the field. First the coach says, "Down," then, "set," then, "go!" He said these words quickly, one right after the other. When he said "go" you ran to the forty-yard line and turned around. Then he made us repeat this back to the goal line. Next we did the same routine to the 50-yard line, then the opposite 40, 30, 20, 10, so that by the end of the drill we had sprinted as far as 100 yards down field… at the end of practice. Guys dropped out like flies, never to return to practice. But I came back. Quitting wasn't an option.

We had one drill called the "crab crawl" where you have to sit down, put your hands behind you to lift your rear off the ground and move forward, backward, and side to side. This meant I would have to do this by using the top of my left arm to balance me out and move up, back and sideways. The thought never crossed my mind to request that I pass on that particular drill. I'm sure the coach running the drill expected me to, but I didn't.

When it was my turn I got down, put my arms behind me and awaited the hand signals that pointed us in the direction the coach wanted us to move. By the time we did these two or three times each, the top of my arm was both black and red. It was red from the blood dripping from the area where the skin had been peeled back and black from the blood mixing with the dirt. After that practice the coach who ran that crab-crawl drill came up to me and said how impressed he was that I did it just like everyone else (well, not exactly like everyone else). We never did the crab crawl again in practice. I'll let that speak for itself.

Once we got our gear things really started to get real. These were two-a-day practices during the peak of summer heat. Admittedly, as I said, I was not as driven this year. Yes, I wanted to play football at this level. I wanted to make the team and play and contribute just as I did in high school. But I did not have the same level of commitment as before. It was as if I did it just to do it. To prove I could do it if I wanted to. Don't get me wrong, I was willing to work hard. It just wasn't the same as it had been in high school.

The other thing we were warned about from the sophomores who had played at LBCC the previous season as freshmen was that when we put on the pads and strapped on our helmets there would be a lot of live hitting-drills and scrimmages. We had done this in high school, but it would be more intense here. With so many quality players there was little to worry about with respect to potential injuries. There were plenty of other guys to take your place if you got hurt. It wasn't malicious on the part of the coaches to feel that way, just the reality of the situation.

Practices continued to be intense leading up to the announcement of the official roster and depth chart, with many days of those brutal hitting-drills and live scrimmages we had been told about. When the depth chart was revealed I was listed as the third-string fullback behind six-foot, four-inch, 235-pound John Kahler, who had been a standout for Wilson in 1966, and Ed Giles, the talented tailback from Long Beach Poly who had starred for the Jackrabbits as a junior and senior in '66 and '67. With all the guys who had originally showed up that first day competing for a roster spot, through all the grueling practices, to emerge as a fullback just behind two outstanding high school football stars who had been All-City and All-League, and in Eddie's case, All-CIF, I was quite pleased with this latest accomplishment.

Keeping my eye on the goal (Long Beach City College in 1968).

There were some very good football players on the 1968 LBCC football team, especially Dennis Dummit, who became a junior college All American and went on to UCLA where he starred at quarterback for head coach Tommy Prothro. We had a successful season and nearly won our conference title. By losing to El Camino Junior College in the final game of the season we lost the division crown by three lousy points. I played often enough and well enough to earn a varsity letter as a freshman. After one particular game in which I played quite a bit, a major-college scout came up to me and told me how impressed he was with my performance. I was blown away. I had every intention of returning the following season to play once again. But destiny had other plans.

―――――

The "Wizard of Westwood," Coach John Wooden, the beyond-legendary college basketball coach whose UCLA Bruin teams achieved immortality by winning ten NCAA National Championships in a 12-year period during his illustrious career there, once said, "Failing to prepare is preparing to fail." That is so true and it doesn't just apply to sports.

During the semester following my first season of football at LBCC I was going through my, "I'm so confused," phase of young adulthood. Not really knowing what I wanted to do with the rest of my life I stopped focusing as I should have on my studies. I worked as a busboy for a time, but mostly I did very little except hang out with a friend, Kirk Smith. Kirk was actually the younger brother of a girl I had a crush on, Shelley, but nothing ever came of that relationship beyond being close friends. Kirk and I drove around in his Volkswagen bus a lot, cruising up and down Pacific Coast Highway to Seal Beach and Huntington Beach during the day on the lookout for girls (always unsuccessfully). We also went to the Los Altos Drive-In Theater and the Circle Drive-In at night, but rarely with actual dates. Mostly we went to watch Sean Connery in *James Bond* movies and other action pictures of the time. We goofed off more than I ever had before or ever want to again. Thankfully, because I had been an athlete, despite its prevalence all around me, I never got into drugs of any kind, not even an occasional hit of grass. To this day I've never experimented with marijuana or any other drug. I can't say the same for alcohol, but I had emphatically said "No" to drugs. I felt like I was going nowhere fast.

Because I lost my focus on my studies my grades suffered so much that I became ineligible to play football for LBCC in 1969. I was very disappointed in myself for allowing this to happen, as it showed a lack of character on my part. I was a far cry from actually being a dolt or lazy, so it was embarrassing to find myself in this position. I might have been able to get one of my grades changed before my downward slide to enable me to become eligible to play football, but after my experience in high school along those lines I wasn't about to attempt that. Instead of giving up on my studies or football for that matter, I continued on at LBCC the next fall, picking up the pace on my studies during that first semester and goofing off considerably less.

I also kept up my football skills by going back to Wilson High School and working out with the varsity during their practices in the afternoons. That started after one afternoon of just hanging out with the team during practice. The players, which included Kirk Smith, looked up to me because the seniors had been sophomores when I was on the varsity team and they admired what I had accomplished while I was a senior and at LBCC. One of their top players, Brian Doheny, became the CIF Player of the Year that season. Somehow I got involved in returning kickoffs and punts that first afternoon and the coaches encouraged me to return the next day. Knowing that I wasn't able to play that season in junior college, they were generous enough to let me work out with the team to stay in shape and prepare myself for the following season at LBCC. Little did I know that an unforeseeable event would soon forever change my life in an unmistakably profound way.

I continued to go to college each weekday that I had classes, worked at Dad's two liquor stores on some evenings and the weekends, and also worked out with the Wilson High School varsity football team. I guess in a way I ended up going full circle, as I now found myself feeling a bit like the team mascot once again, albeit an admired mascot. A better way to look at it was that I was a quasi-coach. It certainly sounds better. Anyway, it was healthy for me to channel my energies in this way and I believe the players and coaches liked having me as an unofficial member of their team as they went about trying to win the Moore League Championship.

During that season I had become a pretty close friend with Lamont Larkin, a young African-American who had transferred to Wilson from Poly and was now playing quarterback on the varsity. He was one of only three or four African-American students at Wilson, while at Poly nearly a third of their student body was black. Lamont and I had been in the same high school fraternity my senior year. He and I decided to go to the Poly vs. Lakewood game because it was on a different night than Wilson's next game and we wanted to scout both teams.

It was at this game that my life was impacted in a way that no other single event had or would. It was destiny. Standing out in front of the refreshment stands some cute girls from Poly came up to say hello to Lamont. He had gone to Franklin Junior High, which fed students to Poly before coming to Wilson and was very popular with everyone, as he was a handsome, polite and kind young gentleman who made friends easily.

Lamont introduced me to the girls. One of them was Kathleen Louise Knauff. Very attractive, I thought, but didn't give it a second thought that night. Then, by "chance" (I actually do not believe in chance meetings or coincidences) I started seeing Kathy at different places; at a party at Lamont's parents' house, other football games, etc. I couldn't get over how attractive she was. She was prettier than any girl I had ever met. At Lamont's party Kathy had been with a guy I knew and I couldn't help watching them together and thinking, "What the heck does she see in this guy?" I left the party early.

I found out later that when I left Kathy asked the guy she was sitting with who I was. He told her I had been a senior at Wilson when they were sophomores and that it was remarkable that I had played varsity football on a championship team. Kathy asked him what was so remarkable about that, lots of guys play football. He said, "Yeah, but, you know, Lynn doesn't have a left hand." She was shocked. I didn't learn about this event until much later. Kathy had met me and then seen me several times by now, and I'd been at this party for a couple of hours, yet she hadn't noticed that I didn't have a left hand. This had happened to me before, and it has happened many times since, but never with such bearing on my life. She became somewhat intrigued about me and was curious as to what kind of person I was.

I then saw Kathy and four of her girlfriends a couple weeks later when Wilson played Poly in a game at Wilson's Stevens Field. I was sitting a couple of rows behind them and alternated between watching the action on the field and staring at the girls, especially Kathy. She turned and saw me and I winked at her. "I never wink at girls," I thought. "What was that about?"

Wilson again defeated Poly that night, but far more importantly, I soon struck up a relationship with this beautiful, intelligent, and interesting young lady who knocked me off my feet. I would never be the same, and I am truly blessed for having met this wonderful girl so many years ago. I asked the girls if they wanted to come to my house following the game and they agreed to, following me home in their car. While at my house we talked and joked and I really enjoyed all the girls' company. Kathy left me her telephone number. The following week, filled with the bursting confidence of a bowl of Jell-O I called Kathy on the phone. After some pleasant small talk I asked her... no, I said to her, "You wouldn't want to go out with me would you?" Who could resist that? To my surprise, Kathy said, yes.

To say that I was "enamored" would be the understatement of a lifetime. I fell head over heels in love with Kathy. She was always in my thoughts and I couldn't wait to see her again. We would talk on the telephone for hours on end. To make a long, but wonderful personal story short, we spent countless hours together whenever possible, especially on Saturday nights after she got off work from the Breakers Hotel in Long Beach. We would eat fast-food from Taco Bell and watch the *Andy Williams Show* on TV. We also went to several high school football games and movies. I proposed to Kathy in December of her senior year in high school. She had just turned 17 in October and I had become 19 just a few weeks before I proposed to her. It sounds beyond implausible, I realize, but the night that I proposed to her following my dad's company Christmas Party at the Long Beach Yacht Club Kathy and I simply knew we were meant to be together for the rest of our lives. When I asked her to marry me, her eyes began welling up with tears. She had a wonderful, loving smile and said, "Yes!"

Kathy and I were married on June 20, 1970 at Holy Innocence Catholic Church in Long Beach, California just three short days after she graduated from high school. It was a beautiful mass and wedding on a stunningly beautiful, sunny summer afternoon in a quaint little church attended by many family and friends. Even some of the players from Wilson's varsity football team came. I arrived about two hours early.

I wasn't anxious to get married or anything like that; of course not. On that special day we began our adventure together that has lasted and thrived for four remarkable decades. I love Kathy more than life itself and she has enriched my life and influenced me in so many ways that words alone are inadequate to explain it here. I owe her more than I will ever be able to repay in so many ways for so very much.

My beautiful bride at 17 years old on June 20, 1970 (I was 19).

After our Honeymoon, which we spent in Mammoth Lakes in Northern California, I went to work nearly full time at Huntington Harbor Liquors, one of the two stores Dad owned and where I had worked off and on over the past year. I had intended to continue attending school at LBCC and even to play football, but soon I felt that in addition to working at Dad's liquor store I wanted to spend as much time as possible with my 17-year old bride. I'll let you figure out why that appealed to me far more than attending classes and football practice. I later came to realize why it was particularly important for me to finish college and get a degree, but at the time it didn't seem all that important.

In January of 1971, God blessed Kathy and me with our first-born child, a son we named Scott Francis Effinger. We gave Scott my dad's father's name as his middle name to honor the grandfather I was never to meet, a heartfelt gesture that Dad greatly appreciated.

I had long hoped that my first born would be a boy, which I guess is not unusual for many men. Before we got married, Kathy and I used to muse about what our son would be like if we were so fortunate to have one. We both envisioned a robustly healthy, tall, handsome, blonde, good-natured boy born with natural, God-given athletic ability. He would have a pleasant disposition, loving personality and more intelligence than we possessed between us (more than me, at least). As you can see we weren't asking for too much, right. Well, with Scott we received our model son. He was a wonderful, happy child who gave us much joy. He would grow to be six-foot, four-inches tall, a tremendous athlete who was (and is) smart as a whip and universally liked by his classmates, teammates and teachers alike in school, and his friends, co-workers and employers today. Still blonde, Scott has become a fine gentleman, loving husband and father who has developed a successful career within the petroleum industry. We could not be more grateful to God for sending him to us.

Before Scott was born, I had fears that our baby might be born with a birth defect. I had been assured more than once by doctors that there was no reason to believe that my children were at any higher risk than all babies of having a birth defect. I wanted to see that for myself. Since technology hadn't produced sonograms as yet, when they told me upon his birth that he was "all there" and that there were no signs of any abnormalities, the relief I felt was beyond description.

Over the years Scott and I grew up together, and he became as big of a sports fan as I was, maybe more. It was a lot of fun teaching him how to play baseball, football, basketball and tennis. When he was only 11 years old he could run pass patterns as well as high school kids. After he developed a killer two-handed backhand stroke in tennis, I enjoyed telling people that I had taught him that, which was good for a laugh each time I brought it up.

In high school Scott played freshman football as a tight end and wide receiver, junior varsity and varsity basketball as a forward, and was on the varsity tennis team all four years. He was named Most Valuable Tennis Player in his senior year. He was a far more gifted athlete than I had been and I was naturally very proud of him. I was especially proud of him for playing varsity basketball, because of all the sports he played; basketball was the most challenging for him. He was tall, but not a natural shooter. But he worked harder at playing basketball than the other sports because it was more challenging. Since the varsity football team was still playing in the playoffs when basketball season commenced, it was believed that the players on the football team who also would be on the varsity basketball team when their playoffs were over would displace some of the starters, including Scott. But, because he worked so hard on his basketball, Scott ended up remaining a starter even when the other players showed up. He gave 100-percent effort at all times, and it showed. I couldn't have been more proud to be his father.

Dad suffered a tremendous setback in business shortly after Kathy and I got married, losing the liquor stores, strip center, and his apartment complex in Garden Grove. It was a protracted, difficult period and a real blow to Dad. The partnership he had entered into turned into a legal nightmare and the outcome was quite unfavorable to say the least. For several weeks thereafter I was out of work. Not a great way to start a marriage. We moved up to Mammoth Lakes where I got a job as a night auditor at a hotel and Kathy got a job as a maid. After several months of this we returned to Long Beach to look for another job for me that was closer to our family members. Kathy's dad then hired me to work for him on a construction project at the Dow Chemical plant in Hawthorne for Plant & Field, an oil refinery construction company. My father-in-law was the job foreman and my first job assignment was that of "fireman." It was my job to use a fire hose to water down the floor surface where we were working as the welders' torch sparks flew all around, because there were live boilers with flammable chemicals surrounding us.

I also did odd jobs around the job site, basically functioning as a laborer. Because I had displayed a stronger work ethic than some of the other younger guys like me I got bumped up to pipefitter's helper with an eye toward being promoted at some point to pipe-fitter status. Pipefitters not only work with small and medium sized pipes, much like a plumber does, they also work with very large pipes. They carefully manipulate these huge steel objects and bring them together, tightly sealing one to another with large bolts that fasten the flanges of each pipe together. Sometimes these flanges bang together quite hard when being swung into place. It is not unheard of for pipefitters to lose fingers and even entire hands in this line of work. This was probably not the ideal profession for someone who is already without two hands. But I needed a job and this was the one that was available to me.

While still on the Dow Chemical project, I was made an insulator. This required me to wrap pipes in aluminum casings with metal strapping and seal the casings with a "mud" made up primarily of asbestos-laden material. Many of the pipes we insulated were hot as hell since Dow decided to fire up the boilers prior to completion of the insulating process. I still have some small burn scars on my arms from this process, but the really slick moment came when one day I was pulling the metal strapping out of a box in which it was coiled, when the coil snagged but my hand kept moving and the palm of my hand was seriously sliced as a result, much like a severe paper cut.

Following completion of the Dow Chemical project I went to work for Plant & Field at an oil refinery in Orange County as an insulator. That job lasted several weeks, but upon completion of our assignment I was laid off and had to wait for another assignment. When a couple of weeks had passed and I wasn't hired back to work I decided to go to the Plant & Field headquarters to pro-actively ask the president of the company if he had any other openings, possibly even a driver's position going from job site to job site on various assignments. I made an appointment to see him and when I entered his office he had a puzzled look on his face. This well-dressed gentleman looked at me curiously from behind his massive desk and incredulously asked, "You were working for us out on the job sites as a pipe-fitters helper and insulator?"

I enthusiastically replied, "Yes, sir, I certainly was and I'm here to see if you have any openings at other sites, because I really need work."

His next words stung me. He said that I couldn't work for his company and shouldn't have when I did, because of the tremendous liability I posed to his company. Had I been more seriously injured than a few burns and a cut palm, I could have sued them big time, which never occurred to me. I just needed to earn a living and those were the jobs for which I had been hired.

As I looked for employment I soon realized that manual labor was going to be out of the question for me.

A liquor store manager with whom I had a job interview questioned my ability to put a six-pack of beer into a tight paper bag, despite having done so hundreds of times when I worked at Dad's stores. I was also denied work at a fast-food restaurant because the manager said the open position required you to slice meat and cheese on a slicing machine and I might have an accident. This happened over and over again. It became quite clear that I was going to have to find some kind of desk job.

That's when I was hired by Frank Higgins at Sun Lumber Company. Frank had known Dad for many years since he was a lumber salesman and Dad was a carpenter in the early 1950s. Sun Lumber Company had a couple of openings for order desk clerk. Following several interviews, the first of which Dad had secured through his friendship but not with a promise to hire me, I was ecstatic to be hired over several candidates, including a recent graduate from USC. This was a real career opportunity and now I had to make the most of it.

Four of us young men were hired at the same time at the still-growing Sun Lumber Company. Dad had instilled in me a strong work ethic through his example and my years working for him in the summers. That and my experiences in other jobs where I performed at a high level caused me to rise steadily over the next three years. I went from order-desk clerk to assistant to the sales manager, to outside contractor lumber salesman. At the age of 23, I was the youngest of twelve outside salesmen. I had a brand new company car, a company-issued gasoline credit card and a whopping $800 per month salary. I had received considerable praise from Frank Higgins and others while in each position and in the first week as salesman sold $500,000 worth of lumber to a company building a large apartment complex in Redondo Beach. That was very exciting! But my life was about to get a whole lot more exhilarating, and more challenging than I could have imagined.

Chapter Ten

The "Impossible" Dream?

"Believe that you will succeed. Believe it firmly, and you will then do what is necessary to bring it about."
— Dale Carnegie

The "Impossible" Dream?

ONE DAY IN EARLY JANUARY of 1974, as I stated in the Preface of this book, I picked up a copy of the Sunday *Long Beach Independent Press - Telegram*, the local newspaper in Long Beach, California where Kathy and I lived and had gone to high school a few years earlier. Within the sports section there was that feature article about Eddie Giles highlighting the fact that he had recently signed as a free agent with Los Angeles Rams.

Still a huge football fan, I read the article with great interest not only because I knew Eddie well, but also because there resided within me a lingering fixation that I had not reached my full potential as a football player. I harbored a belief that I could still play, despite not having done so in several years. Kathy and I had a three-year-old son and she was pregnant with our second child. I was working as an outside contractor lumber salesman for Sun Lumber Company. It was a good job and I was working toward getting into management at some point in the future.

The real significance attached to having read the article about Eddie was that I suddenly, inexplicably had a flash of inspiration. I got this bold idea that if I worked harder than I ever had to get into the best physical shape of my life and had the help of some kind of publicity campaign I would be able to play semi-pro football the following season. My plan was to perform at the highest possible level and earn a tryout with an NFL team. I believed that were I to pull this off I could prove to others that through hard work, determination and perseverance anyone could overcome obstacles in their path to achieve greater success than anyone dreamed possible. I became quite animated about this and Kathy knew I was as serious about this as anything I had ever been up to this moment.

What convinced Kathy to get behind my idea and give me her complete support was when I said, "This is how I can fulfill the responsibility that Coach Crutchfield had wanted to instill in me." I believed it with all my heart. I committed to accomplishing this unlikely, improbable if not impossible dream right then and there. Another driving force once I made the commitment to pursue this goal was that since I had conceived it I *had* to move forward because I didn't want to grow old and wonder, "what if?" A burning desire and passion to achieve this goal was born.

Semi-pro football, sometimes referred to as minor league football, has been played around the country for decades, usually in the shadows because of the massive media exposure and popularity of the National Football League. In eastern and southern states semi-pro football draws significant crowds to their games in areas where no NFL team is located nearby. In California, semi-pro football tended to be sparsely attended or even followed because of the competing professional, college and high school sports and other activities readily available throughout the state. Particularly in Southern California where we had the L.A. Rams, USC and UCLA football, the Dodgers, the Angels, and the Lakers, just to name a few. In addition, in 1974 the World Football League had just been created and we had one of their franchises, the Southern California Sun, coached by the legendary Tom Fears, located in Anaheim.

The "Impossible" Dream?

Semi-pro football teams are largely populated by players of widely varying backgrounds, levels of football experience, skills and talent. Some have played in the NFL or Canadian Football League or had once tried out, were on the pro's taxi squads or just had one shot at training camp. Others had played at major colleges or universities. Still others had only played a year or two in junior college or high school. Some had played while in the service. The Marine Corps, for example had a team. A few had played football on prison teams! It was not unheard of for some guys to try out who had never played organized football at any level. That's one of the great aspects of semi-pro football; it was and is an outlet for guys who love playing football to have an opportunity to do so once their college eligibility had expired, as mine had. And sometimes semi-pro football players had been seen by pro scouts and signed to play professionally. It didn't happen often, but it did happen.

The very next morning after setting my goal I began pursuing it by running three blocks from our apartment down to Wilson High School. I then jogged a couple of miles around the track which surrounded the football field where I had played throughout high school. I joined a health club that afternoon and started lifting weights again. I began running in the mornings before going to work and worked out in the gym in the early evenings after work. I didn't tell anyone at Sun Lumber Company what I was doing yet, mainly because I didn't want my boss to think I wasn't focused on my job responsibilities. But also because I didn't want anyone to try to tell me I had gone nuts. I did this for several weeks, lost several pounds and began running stadium steps and wind sprints as well as running laps in the morning.

Part of my game plan included generating some publicity about what I was attempting to accomplish. The whole point was to spread the word about my goals for the reasons mentioned above. It was also necessary, in my opinion, because to even get a tryout with a semi-pro football team with my limited credentials was going to be difficult in the extreme. If the owner and coaches of the Orange County Rhinos, the team I was hoping to earn a tryout with believed that I had the requisite skills and a burning desire to prove myself, they might possibly be more open to giving me a shot. Publicity would help me establish my credentials.

After I had been working out on my own for several weeks, I wrote down what I was trying to accomplish and took that piece of paper with me to the *Long Beach Independent Press - Telegram*. Hank Hollingworth was a featured sports writer for our local newspaper. I first met him when I attended the Long Beach Century Club awards dinner as a senior in high school. He had been the emcee for that dinner and knew full well who I was and for what reason I had been honored that evening.

At the front desk of the newspaper offices I asked if I could see Mr. Hollingworth. The receptionist called upstairs to ask if I could come up and Hollingworth said, okay. I took the elevator to the second floor and went to where Hollingworth was sitting behind large glass windows. I sat down across the desk from him on the edge of the chair, leaning forward and began relaying to him what I was doing, hoped to accomplish, and why. He was mostly engaged with listening to me, but also preoccupied a bit because he didn't have much time to complete that day's column. He thanked me for sharing my goals with him and said he'd like to write a little story about it for the paper. He said he would be calling me soon on the telephone to interview me. I thanked him and went on my way, as excited as ever.

I was energized as I left his office and returned to Sun Lumber. I called Kathy from work to tell her I had just taken another step toward achieving my goal. I told her I expected to have a pretty brief news story appear in the paper after Hollingworth interviewed me, but I knew any amount of publicity would be good publicity. She was almost as excited as I was.

In mid-February, I was down at Long Beach State College one afternoon doing some running on my own. While there I came across a former Wilson High graduate, Jeff Severson, who had been a senior when I was a junior and we had been in the same high school fraternity, Sigma Chi Epsilon. Jeff was on the team at LBCC when I played there and he was a star defensive back. He had then transferred to Long Beach State on a football scholarship and became a standout performer there for the next two years. As a senior he tied the single-season collegiate record for interceptions with 13. He was later drafted by George Allen, head coach of the Washington Redskins in 1971, made the taxi squad his first year and then played on the Skin's special teams squad in 1972. That was the year the Redskins lost to the undefeated Miami Dolphins in the Super Bowl in January of 1973. Making the Redskins was quite an admirable feat for Jeff because Allen didn't like rookies. He preferred instead to sign veteran players who ascribed to his, "The Future is Now," philosophy. Jeff was traded following the Super Bowl in early '73 to the Houston Oilers, where he played defensive back and returned punts during the 1973 season.

Jeff had always encouraged me to do my best on the football field and applauded me when I performed well, even in practice. He could be critical of me as well when I made mistakes, but always in a positive way. I looked up to him as a surrogate brother in many ways. After I told him about my mission he praised me for setting my goal and said, "There's a bunch of us from different NFL teams who are coming down here each night and on Saturday mornings to run pass patterns together, why don't you join us?"

He didn't have to ask me twice. I was thrilled that he would ask me to do that and couldn't wait to come out the next evening, which I did. Now, here I was, this former high school football player who only played one year of college football, in junior college no less, running pass patterns with players from the NFL; Harold Jackson, Joe Sweet and Lawrence McCutcheon of the L.A. Rams, Miron Pottios of the Redskins, Terry Metcalf, a former star at Long Beach State who was with the St. Louis Cardinals, and other well-known players at the time. Also there each night was Dennis Dummit, my friend from Wilson and LBCC who later played quarterback at UCLA. He had recently been signed by the Hawaiian franchise of the WFL. There were others at practices who were currently playing in the NFL or who were going to be trying out for teams in either the NFL or the WFL. There was a different group each night, but Jeff was almost always there, as were Dennis and I. From that first night on I never missed a workout in over four months.

On one particular Saturday morning with strong winds blowing caused by what is known in Southern California as "Santa Ana conditions," where high pressure brings in hot, gusting wind blowing offshore from the desert, only Dennis and I showed up to work out. Dennis had me run pass patterns from the wide receiver, tight end and running back positions. He said we couldn't stop our workout until I had caught two passes in a row from each position, from both sides of the ball, meaning right side and left side. In these windy, gusting conditions this task was made even more challenging for this one-handed receiver, but we got through it and I was quite proud of myself for having accomplished Dennis's assignment.

Things just seemed to be lining up, like the proverbial "sun, the moon and the stars." It was beginning to feel apparent to me that all was meant to be. When President Nixon eliminated "standard time," keeping daylight savings time in place through the fall and winter months that year to help save energy following the OPEC oil embargo, it meant daylight lasted longer. This enabled us to work out at Long Beach State deeper into the early evening hours. I loved every second of these workouts and learned a lot from these professional players.

Just a week or so after I had met with Hank Hollingworth, he called me on the phone at work and asked me a few questions for clarification, then told me to come to the paper the next day to be photographed. I went downtown to the *Press - Telegram* the following morning and sat on a stool while a photographer took a few shots and then I stopped by and said hello to Hank. He told me the story in the paper would come out on February 24th so I could buy a paper that morning. I thanked him again for his time and for agreeing to write a little story about my quest.

I had a hard time sleeping the night before the story was to appear in the paper. On the morning of February 24th I got up really early and went to the nearest 7-11 convenience store and saw the papers weren't there yet. I returned a while later to find a full newspaper rack. I put in my quarter, fumbling nervously, and took out... all the papers. I know, I know, it was wrong, but I have a lot of relatives. I hoped the *Press - Telegram* would understand; Bad boy.

I didn't wait to get home before opening up one of my ill-gotten newspapers to see what Hank had written. I was only expecting a few brief sentences, or perhaps a paragraph or two. I would have been happy with anything. But to my amazement the biggest headline on the front page of the sports section declared, "**Effinger rates pro tryout on his desire and courage.**" The story took up two large columns on the front page and jumped to the inside. I was completely blown away. I couldn't have paid to have so many complimentary things said about me and what I was trying to accomplish.

I returned home shortly and showed Kathy the newspaper. She was thrilled, too. Another piece of my plan fell into place. I called Hank early that morning and thanked him again. He told me to feel free to send him notes about any progress I might make towards achieving my goal.

But then he said he hoped that I wouldn't be too disappointed if things didn't work out the way I wanted them to, as my quest was a long shot. That was the same reaction that many people, even some of my family members expressed to me when they learned of my mission. I thanked him for his concern and assured him that I would make things happen just as I had envisioned them. That is a point worth making here – I could literally visualize myself playing football for the Rhinos and getting a tryout with a team in the NFL. It was very real to me. Because of this, I never doubted that I would succeed – Yes I can, yes I will, just watch me.

After the story ran, it was going to be a tad more difficult to keep my mission a secret from my boss and coworkers at Sun Lumber Company. When I arrived at the office that morning the receptionist and our accountant came up to me, gave me hugs and with tears in their eyes told me how proud they both were of me. Others in the office were less tearful, but equally complimentary and encouraging. I received quite a bit of positive feedback from these wonderful people. My boss, Frank Higgins, was even positive, not once asking me to explain how I intended to stay productive at work while pursuing my "impossible" dream.

When I arrived at Long Beach State for pass-pattern workouts early that evening, most all of the players on hand, especially Jeff and Dennis were also very gracious in acknowledging that they read the article and praised my motives. I was fired up that night, I can tell you. Everywhere I went for the next couple of weeks, people would stop me and tell me they had read Hank's article and that they were behind me 100 percent. I knew publicity would help, but I hadn't realized just how many people read the local newspaper back then. It was a great feeling to know I had the support of friends and acquaintances, and even many who didn't know me. I derived much strength from this support. Even the guys at my favorite pizzeria, Larizza's Pizza on Seventh Street in Long Beach, made a big deal out of having read the article and said that they were all pulling for me!

Soon after the article hit the street I sent a letter to Bob Flowers, the owner of the Rhinos, requesting a tryout. I was hoping he too had read the article, which he had. He replied to my request by sending me a letter with the dates he expected to begin holding tryouts, the times and the location, which was to be Chapman College in the City of Orange. He formally invited me to try out for the 1974 Southern California Rhinos of the California Football League (Flowers had recently changed the name from Orange County Rhinos because so many players came from Long Beach, which is in Los Angeles County). Tryouts were to commence in July. The California Football League would be playing games from August through early November to get a jump on the NFL and collegiate football seasons to try to generate attendance. I was getting closer to achieving my goal.

I continued my workout regime of running laps, stadium steps and wind sprints in the morning, lifting weights in the afternoon and running pass patterns in the early evenings week after week, month after month. One day we saw an announcement in the paper that the Southern California Sun of the fledgling WFL was going to be holding an open quarterback tryout session at the Santa

Ana Bowl football stadium in Orange County the following Saturday morning. A couple of us who were working out at Long Beach State who hadn't yet signed with any pro teams thought we should go, just for the heck of it.

When we arrived at the stadium about 80 or so "prospects" were there awaiting instructions on how to participate. It was a quarterback tryout, but they needed receivers. That's why we attended. There were a few calisthenics to get us warmed up and some drills to test for coordination and agility. The main purpose of the workout was for receivers to run various pass patterns while the quarterback hopefuls threw us passes, or I guess I should say they "attempted" to throw us passes. They weren't the most accurate passers I'd ever seen. Having run pass patterns at Long Beach State for many weeks paid off, as my routes were crisp and clean. I caught far more passes than I missed, often diving for errant throws.

The final drill of that mostly uneventful morning was simply the 40-yard dash. If you ran it under a certain time you would be asked to stay for the afternoon session, if you didn't you were simply excused. It was an easy way to eliminate the vast majority of participants. I barely missed hitting the required time and was therefore done with this workout. I wasn't at all disappointed because I had no expectation of getting signed by the Sun as a wide receiver. I am an optimist, but also a realist. It was more of a test to see where I was in relationship with other potential players.

As I was walking out of the stadium, a young man came up to me and introduced himself. His name was Earl Gustkey. He said he was a reporter for the *Los Angeles Times* and asked if he could interview me. Because of the reaction I had received from Hank's piece, I agreed. More exposure would be a good thing, especially in the heavily read *L.A. Times*, one of the nation's great newspapers back then, when newspapers were still relevant.

Gustkey's article was mostly complimentary, as portended by its headline; **One-Handed Back Is Determined.** The article then went on to say, "Lynn Effinger is exactly one arm's length away from being a pro football prospect." Not altogether positive, but at least it didn't say I was one can short of a six pack or that both oars didn't reach the water. Gustkey also said in his piece, "He seemed to be in good condition and he showed good running speed," and "He wasn't short-changed on determination, however. At the end of Saturday's tryout, he was covered in mud, from diving after poorly thrown passes." At the conclusion of the article he wrote, "After the five-hour tryout session, Effinger left for Cal State Long Beach… to work out," which I felt was testimony to my dedication to pursuing my goal. KABC-TV News ran a story that evening on their nightly broadcast and there I was on television running pass patterns for all to witness.

The day after this story ran in the *L.A. Times*, Frank Higgins called me into his office. By this time I was spending a tremendous amount of time working out throughout the day. My sales production had fallen a bit during this time and I figured I was going to be called on the carpet. I felt guilty about it, but I wasn't going to let anything keep me from achieving my goal. Instead of lecturing or admonishing me, Frank asked me what I thought of the *Times* article. I said I was okay with most of it but thought the writer pre-judged my chances to get an NFL tryout just because I was born without a left hand. He then asked me, "Lynn, do you believe in God?"

I looked him straight in the eyes and replied, "Yes sir, absolutely, and I firmly believe that everyone is put here on earth for a purpose. Mine is to pursue this goal and successfully achieve it so that my accomplishment can serve as a positive example to others, no matter what anybody says or believes, because I am determined to make it happen."

Frank didn't say another word. He just smiled at me and nodded his head as if to say he understood completely. And for the next several months he never, ever asked me where I was or what I was doing, or how many sales leads I was working on. Nothing, until I had completed my mission. I will be forever grateful to Frank Higgins and his superior, Miles Davidson, for allowing me to pursue my goal with their unspoken blessing. Without that level of support from my employer it would have been much more difficult to accomplish my mission. Things just seemed meant to be... some more.

Subsequent to the publication of the *Times* article I was also featured in the *Orange County Register* and was interviewed by KNX radio in Los Angeles. Hank Holingworth continued to chronicle my progress as well, which was giving me the publicity I knew would help spread the word about what I was trying to accomplish and why.

Training camp for the Rhinos commenced just after the 4th of July holiday. When I showed up that first evening along with dozens and dozens of other hopefuls, the coaches and most of the players knew who I was and about my motivation for being there. I had successfully set the stage for my tryout with the Rhinos. It was gratifying to know a couple of the players who were there, like Buster LaCoste and Preston Sadler who I had played alongside at LBCC, and Kerry Stewart, whom I had known since junior high school.

The Rhinos owner, Bob Flowers, introduced himself and the coaches. Our head coach was Al Williams. Williams had coached semi-pro football for years and his teams had actually scrimmaged the Dallas Cowboys a couple of times in the past when they trained at Cal Lutheran College in Thousand Oaks, California. Our other coach was Cal Waterhouse. Flowers then welcomed us all to the Rhinos training camp. All the players introduced themselves to one another that first night and explained what their background and experience level was with respect to football. There were quite a few players who were returning after playing previously for the Rhinos. The coaches talked about their expectations of us, what our practice schedule would be, when our games would be and who the opponents were. Our first game was only three weeks away, so we had to get started right away.

As practice got underway I volunteered to help lead calisthenics and did so with two other players. I remembered what Eddie Meador had said at that Optimist Club breakfast in 1965 before I entered high school and put his advice to work from the get-go. After those exercises and a few drills were completed we all ran the 40-yard dash for time. I ran a 4.8 that night, which back then was about average for a fullback, but not as fast as some of my competitors for the starting fullback position, of which there were several.

One of the guys I quickly made friends with was Steve Corwin, a halfback who had played football for El Modina High School in Villa Park, California and Fullerton State College. Steve was a great guy and a very good halfback. He was a little shorter than me but built rock solid and fast. He had a good sense of humor and we enjoyed hanging out together. I looked forward to getting to play alongside him at some point, were I to make the team as anticipated.

We were given playbooks on the second night of practice so that we could study them and begin running plays as soon as possible. Practice uniforms and equipment soon followed that first Saturday. The next few practices got more intense as the hitting commenced. These guys could hit hard, and loved doing so. It had been a while for me since hitting and getting hit, and being tackled. I had rarely been hit by players who were this big and fast. It didn't take long to get into the swing of things, however, and I gave as well or better than I received.

After three weeks of practice the coaches announced the official roster and gave us the depth chart. Because I had worked so hard over the previous months in preparation for trying out for the Rhinos, then went the extra mile in each practice session as Eddie Meador had suggested, I not only made the team, I was named starting fullback for our first game against the Las Vegas Casinos. The game would be played the following week at the University of Nevada Las Vegas Stadium. Another milestone successfully reached.

The bus ride we took as a team to Vegas was more eventful than we would have liked. Out in the middle of the California desert, in early August, our bus's air conditioning unit failed. It was over 100 degrees outside and miserable in that bus the rest of the way. Talk about malodorous!

Upon arrival at the stadium we cooled off inside the cafeteria and had a decent pre-game team meal. We lounged around a bit and had a brief team meeting. Then we put on our gear and game uniforms and went onto the field for pre-game warm-ups. It didn't take very long to get warm. It was dark by then, but on the field the temperature was 110 degrees. The enthusiastic crowd was already growing. Although not a sell-out, it would end up a good-sized throng.

The Las Vegas Casinos were in a different league than us and had actually been playing their season for many weeks. This was our first game. Eddie Lebaron, who had played quarterback for many years as a star in the NFL, was the Casino's general manager. Their head coach, Karl Sweetan had been a backup quarterback behind Roman Gabriel of the Los Angeles Rams in the 1960s. Their team boasted several former NFL and Canadian Football League players. Their uniforms were black and white with a logo on their black helmets that was identical to the Chicago Bears. These guys were big, fast and intimidating. We knew we were in for a tough night. We soon enough found out just how tough; after a couple of "streakers" mooned the crowd, of course. Even back then, people were a little crazy in Vegas.

We lost that first pre-season game by a score of 66-0. They had a blazingly fast tailback that scored five times!

The "Impossible" Dream?

Our defense was nowhere to be found. We should have looked in the same place as our offense, because we weren't there either. We got pounded. I don't think I averaged over 1.5 yards per carry that night and injured my right knee a bit towards the end of the game. It was clear that we needed a lot of work to improve all aspects of our game. We needed to play better as a team. There was no excuse for our pitiful collective performance.

After the blowout we stayed in Sin City at a cheap motel that night. I hobbled around as best I could with Steve Corwin and a couple of other players for several hours in one of the casinos. We drowned our sorrows and went back to our rooms and crashed. It was already the next day. When we woke up a few hours later our bodies were battered and bruised, but not as much as our egos. What a lousy ride back to California. At least our driver had fixed the air conditioning unit.

Just one night after returning from Las Vegas, on August 3, 1974 Kathy said it was time to go to the hospital to deliver our second child. I gathered up her bag and helped her down the stairs to our car and we took off for Long Beach Memorial Hospital across town. Kathy strongly suggested that I stop hitting every bump there was in the road, which was odd to me because I didn't feel any of them. After getting her checked in, Kirk, and my sister-in-law Kaye, Kathy's longtime friend arrived at the hospital. A while later an intern said it was a false alarm and sent Kathy and the rest of us home. Kathy thought for sure he was mistaken, but we returned to our apartment.

It was fairly late in the evening. Kirk and Kaye and I decided to have a glass or two of wine out in the living room in a wildly insensitive display of inconsideration while Kathy was lying down on our bed... but not for long. She soon emerged from the bedroom and said, "We're going back," in a tone that left no room for negotiation. Back into the car and off to the hospital we went again. I dropped Kathy off inside the emergency room and left to park the car. I hadn't been gone long at all, but upon my return they told me they had already wheeled her upstairs to the delivery room. In what seemed like only moments later a nurse came to me and said, "Congratulations, it's a baby girl!" Always trust a mother's instincts. Diana Lynn Effinger was to become my spoiled little angel from that moment on. Our little family was now complete; one boy and one girl. Perfect, we thought.

As our football practices progressed, it was clear to anyone paying attention that we weren't jelling together as a unit. It seemed like we were all a bunch of individuals out there freelancing on our own, not really becoming a cohesive team. In 1974 race relations were not that great. It hadn't been that long since there had been riots in Watts and similar events in other major cities across the nation in the mid-and-late sixties. Living conditions and opportunities for blacks and Hispanics had not improved as much as they felt they should have in the mid-seventies. This helped to create an environment on our football team where the whites hung out with the whites, the blacks with the blacks and the Hispanics with other Hispanics.

Because of our collective disunity, I called a meeting before our next practice out on the football field to try to flush this out. I stood in front of everyone and acknowledged that we were all there for different reasons. We were all motivated to play and win, but we couldn't and wouldn't unless we all hung together, played together and became a truly unified team. Our team goal of winning a championship had to come first. If we were successful as a team our individual goals would be easier to achieve. Others expressed their feelings, as well. We all agreed that it was in our collective best interests to put our differences aside. We needed to get to know each other better, hang together before, during and after practice and be supportive of each other in any way that we could. It was like turning on a light switch. From that night on we were in this thing together and never wavered from our loyalty and support for one another despite the many challenges that came our way.

I was very pleased by the outcome of my being the catalyst for bringing us together. We all believed that our chances of winning a championship could only get better as a result. Sometimes you just have to step up and lead. I don't remember exactly where or when, but I read once that in life you can lead, follow, or get out of the way. I choose to lead.

Our second game two weeks after the Vegas game was in British Columbia, Canada against the Vancouver Barons.

The game was played at the B.C. Lions stadium and was fairly well attended. We had played on plush AstroTurf in Las Vegas but the "carpet" covering the field in this old stadium was tired, worn out and the seams had exposed zippers. Getting tackled and landing on this surface felt as if we were playing on asphalt in the middle of the street. Although we lost the game, we played much better. My knee had recuperated and I again started at fullback. I ran well with the ball and blocked soundly. More importantly, as a team, we seemed to be making progress.

At the post-game party we had with players from both teams and many of their fans, I received quite a few compliments for the way I had played. That was very gratifying, but I hoped we would start winning soon.

We lost our first two California Football League games by small margins against the East L.A. Ramblers and the Sacramento Statesman but we had just picked up a couple more players that had recently been released by NFL teams. One such player, Craig Schneider, was a 225-pound linebacker who made it to the final cut with the Miami Dolphins, a team that had posted a perfect season the year before. Craig was a great addition to our defense, as were the other players we added to the team.

After losing those first two league games we went on a seven-game winning streak, defeating the Lancaster Sidewinders twice, the San Fernando Lancers twice, the Thousand Oaks Kings twice, and the East L.A. Ramblers. Our defense became so strong by mid-season they were scoring almost as many points as our offense each week. These impressive consecutive wins brought us to a showdown with the Sacramento Statesman on the final week of the season. The game against the Statesmen, who had narrowly defeated us on their home field several weeks prior, would decide the California Football League Championship. Because I believed that this game would possibly draw the largest crowd that season, I had another idea to help further publicize what I was trying to accomplish. It would also help a worthy cause and further boost ticket sales. I asked the Rhinos' owner, Bob Flowers, if we could divide the net proceeds for the championship game between himself and the March of Dimes, fully explaining the rationale for doing so. Bob was notoriously, shall we say, "tight" but he recognized opportunity when it stared him in the face.

I chose the March of Dimes because they were the only charitable organization in America at the time that had accomplished its original mission. They helped to eradicate polio in the United States in the 1950s. As a victim of this scourge himself, President Franklin D. Roosevelt had helped to create the March of Dimes. The organization's mission following their first success was now to help fight birth defects. This was a mission close to my heart, and another reason for choosing to support them.

I told Bob that I would create posters and flyers to help promote the fundraising game, speak at civic clubs and talk to reporters to help promote ticket sales. I also told him I would personally have special tickets printed and then distribute them to key sites such as sporting goods stores and other retailers who might be willing to help promote the game. Bob didn't take long to agree to my plan (especially the part about my paying to have the tickets printed). I immediately got to work promoting the game as a fundraiser after receiving permission from the Executive Directors of the Orange County and Long Beach Chapters of the March of Dimes to use their name in such an endeavor.

Flowers arranged for us to hold the championship game at the Santa Ana Bowl instead of the Chapman College stadium where we normally played our home games. It was a much larger venue and therefore had the capacity to seat more fans. Because the game would now be a fundraiser, stadium officials cut the Rhinos a special deal for renting the stadium to help ensure we would raise more money for the March of Dimes.

Competing for a paying audience in Southern California on a Saturday night, even when raising money for charity, would be difficult at best. The people at the March of Dimes, however, understood that this game and all the publicity created would help raise awareness within the community about their mission. Whatever monies were raised would be icing on the cake. They mostly were being supportive of *me* because they appreciated my enthusiasm about the mission of the March of Dimes.

I had successfully prepared myself to try out for the Rhinos. I then worked harder than I ever had to make the team, which I did, becoming the team's starting fullback. I played well and had contributed to our team's successful season up to this point, publicizing my progress whenever possible. We were now in a position to win the California Football League Championship in our final game of the year; A game that would help raise money for a worthy charitable organization. And get me another step closer to achieving my goal. Destiny was calling.

Chapter Eleven

A Dream Come True

*"Plant the seed in your mind; cultivate thoughts that anticipate achievement.
Believe in yourself as being capable of overcoming obstacles and weaknesses."*

– Norman Vincent Peale

D URING THE TWO-WEEK PERIOD LEADING up to the championship game with the Sacramento Statesmen I had been invited to be the guest speaker at the Lion's Club, and Rotary Club in Long Beach. Although I was not a polished public speaker I agreed to attend and speak about the upcoming game to help promote the March of Dimes fundraiser as I had said I would in the stories that appeared in the newspapers.

To be perfectly honest, I had always been petrified of speaking in front of people, even in a classroom full of kids I knew quite well to give an oral report of one kind or another. I didn't like to be stared at and just wasn't comfortable having all eyes fixated on me... and my left arm (whether anyone was actually staring at my arm or not, it always seemed that all eyes were pointed to one spot). I was usually home in bed, "sick," on the mornings I was supposed to give my oral report. I generally had a mysterious but debilitating illness that certainly no doctor would be able to diagnose. This "illness" led to receiving an inevitable "F" for not completing the speaking assignment. This did not endear me to my parents.

This went on for years. But one day in the ninth grade our English teacher, Mrs. Milkes, who I liked very much, gave us our next major assignment. She said, "Class, your next assignment is to give an oral report." After they had revived me (just kidding), I also heard her follow up with, "You may choose any subject you wish to talk about." Well, I finally decided after hearing her follow-up sentence that since I was about to go on to high school I had better stop wimping out and come up with a subject that

I could talk about in an oral report. Suddenly it came to me in a flash what my report should be about! I then made my decision as to what my subject would be and wrote down my thoughts on 3x5 index cards to serve as notes for my address. On the day that I was to give my oral report I actually showed up in class, ready with my 3x5 index cards containing my notes firmly in hand. I was prepared.

When I was called upon by Mrs. Milkes to give my oral report, I slowly rose from my desk chair and walked to the front of the class, confidently. As I arrived at the appointed spot at the front of the classroom I turned and faced my classmates. I stood up in an erect fashion, lowered my voice like the broadcasters I often heard on the radio, and calmly, but forcefully announced to my audience, "Class, what I am about to tell you today is… why I hate to give oral reports."

I knew my subject intimately. Because I had written down my thoughts as notes and confidently delivered my oral report I received an "A+" grade from Mrs. Milkes. And that was the beginning of a dramatic turnaround that was enhanced by taking a drama class in high school for which I also received an A grade for the semester. I began to not only feel more comfortable in front of people and speaking to them, I rather enjoyed it as I became more proficient at it. Not polished, but proficient and more relaxed.

When I worked for Sun Lumber Company I had been selected to participate with a select few employees in a special management training program. As a member of the group going through the program I was required to give several oral presentations. This also helped me improve as a speaker.

I discovered while addressing the attendees at the two civic club meetings to promote the championship football game that I had inspired the audience. When I spoke to them about my passion for achieving my personal mission, what I had done so far to accomplish it, the desire I had to support the March of Dimes, they applauded enthusiastically. A new and exciting way for me to continue to fulfill my "Responsibility" after playing football was revealed to me. I have ever since given motivational presentations at schools, churches, civic clubs, trade associations, corporations and other organizations across the country. Not only did I lose the fear of public speaking over time, I came to enthusiastically seek out more and more opportunities to give motivational presentations. I didn't find motivational speaking as much as it found me.

The local newspapers ran stories about the championship game that helped promote the fundraiser, just as we had hoped. That increased the excitement of my teammates for playing this last, pivotal contest of our season. Hank Hollingworth wrote, among other things:

> The Southern California Rhinos, currently leading the California Football League, will play the Sacramento Statesmen at the Santa Ana Bowl and the beneficiary will be the March of Dimes of Long Beach. For this engagement, they hope to get a crowd.

The game is significant not only from the charity angle, but also because it is [another] step in the 'Magnificent Plan' of Lynn Effinger, the young Long Beach football player who was born with only part of an arm – no hand – and on pure guts made the Rhinos starting lineup as fullback.

When Lynn made up his mind last February to play pro football somewhere this season, he came to us and detailed his strategy, which was laudable, but hardly workable – or so we thought – because who wants a one-armed ball carrier?

Rhinos President, Bob Flowers, hopes the charity affair will lure more than the usual corporal's guard that steadfastly turns out for Rhinos games.

"I hope we can draw a crowd because of Lynn Effinger's work," said Flowers. "He has been a fine addition to the Rhinos and is an example of intestinal fortitude surpassed by no one. He has averaged four yards per carry, which is darned good for any fullback."

Southern California Rhinos and March of Dimes PR Photo with me and Victor Miller.

We no doubt received better coverage than we otherwise would have because of my initiative, which was gratifying to me. But not as much as having a P.R. photo taken with Victor Miller, the 11-year old poster child for the local

March of Dimes chapters. Victor had been born with spina bifida, a part of a group of birth defects called neural tube defects, a crippling disease that often means a reduced life expectancy. He was a cute, energetic little boy who thought it was cool that I was able to play football. We hit it off together right from the start. The March of Dimes arranged for their photographer, Jasper Nutter, to take the photo, which we used in conjunction with all of our press releases. Prior to the night of the game, which Victor and his parents would be attending with him, I bought him a youth football helmet. I painted it yellow, put two blue stripes down the middle and placed Rhinos logo decals on each side, just like the helmets all of us players wore. I gave it to him just before pre-game warm-ups and he was so excited it gave me goose bumps watching him put it on.

On that cool, crisp Saturday evening of November 8, 1974 during pre-game warm-ups we all knew that we were in for a rough battle with this opponent. They were big, they were aggressive, and they wanted to prove to us they were the better team. Of course we believed we were better even though we had lost to them at the beginning of the season. We were fired up during warm-ups and ran our drills and mock-plays with fierce determination to be at our very best. Victor wore his helmet out to the middle of the field for the coin toss with the referee and team captains, of which I was one, and didn't take it off all night.

The game itself proved to be every bit as demanding as we had expected. Steve Corwin and I both started the game in the backfield as we had in every game but one that season. We platooned our backs and receivers throughout each game, meaning we shuttled in fresh players from time to time to keep an edge on the defense. I hated coming out whenever I did because I always wanted to be in the game, somewhat selfishly I must admit. But it was my competitive spirit that made me constantly want to be on the field. No doubt the other backs felt the same when I was in the game instead of them. Had any of us been far superior to the others we might not have platooned our backs and receivers so often, but that was not the case so this made sense to the team. The team's performance is what mattered most.

Most of us players had been quite anxious to get the game underway. We were exceedingly confident of our chances for victory and winning the league championship, but there were 60 minutes of grueling football to be played. No more talk and no more hype. After the opening kickoff the game progressed with neither team seeming to have a clear-cut advantage over the other. On one particularly hard hit by our right cornerback, Bobby McClure, he stood over the receiver who dropped the ball after the collision and yelled out, "You couldn't catch a cold!" This fired us up even more. Back and forth we went for two quarters. Everybody on each team played with the kind of intensity and singleness of purpose that you would expect during a championship game.

Trailing 7-3 at the half, we took to the air to gradually gain control of the game in the third quarter. Quarterback Paul Eddy passed 31 yards to tight end Mike Gregg late in the third period to gain the lead at 9-7. We then successfully converted the extra point to go up 10-7 with the outcome of the game still on the line. On an off-tackle play I took the handoff and burst through the line nearly untouched and broke behind one of Corwin's always-reliable blocks on the outside linebacker. I saw nothing but daylight and turned on what speed I possessed. Just as I thought I would break away, the ball was jarred from my right arm as I cut to the center of the field. I couldn't believe it! On what would have been my longest run of the season I had broken clear, only to lose the ball and the Statesmen recovered it at midfield; Damn!

Back on the sidelines Steve Corwin tried his best to console me but I was ticked at myself for letting this happen, especially on this night, in this crucial game. Our defense held the Statesmen to three downs and they punted the ball. Bobby McClure ran the punt to our 36-yard line. I went back into the game. On the first play after we received the punt, Mike Cochran called a pass play. When the ball was snapped the defensive end came blasting through the line outside our tackle. He was all mine. I hit him so hard he flipped over the top of me. Mike got the ball off to wide receiver, Stan Chapman who ran for 33 yards. We continued to drive up the field with a punishing combination of running and passing plays.

Coach Williams chose to bring in fresh backs during the middle of this crucial drive and I watched from the sidelines as our offense kept driving toward the goal line. As the team got inside the ten-yard line and it was third-and-goal-to-go, we all heard Paul Eddy, our quarterback during this drive, yelling something. He was calling my name! He wanted me in the game as we attempted to score a decisive touchdown that could cement our hold on the game. I ran onto the field as fast as I could, not waiting for

A Dream Come True

Coach Williams to say a word. Paul called 31 Power Dive, which featured the fullback (me) running with the ball off the right guard's lead block. Our veteran right guard, Charlie Shaw, was over 40-years old and had played for several years for the Cleveland Browns in the NFL and had actually blocked for my hero, the legendary Jim Brown, so this was going to be our best opportunity for me to score.

Paul Eddy started calling signals, "Ready... Red 36, Red 36... set... Hut!" On his command we all drove forward in unison, I took the ball cleanly from Paul and hit the line hard. But Charlie had not been able to move the defender he was supposed to block and I only gained one yard. Now it's fourth and goal. We would normally have tried for a field goal to get three more points on the board in this situation, but Paul waved off the kicking team, choosing instead to run 31 Power Dive once again; A gutsy call.

After Paul called the play in the huddle he said, "Let's get Lynn in there, guys... break!" We all echoed, "Break!" Then we broke the huddle, turned and faced our enemy on the line of scrimmage. Charlie turned to me and said, "Follow me kid, I got this guy's number this time."

Again Paul called the signals, "Ready... Blue 26, Blue 26... set... Hut!"

We drove forward again, but with an even greater sense of purpose. Charlie blasted the lineman in front of him and I crashed into the line behind him and felt it give way as I pounded ahead, pumping my legs until I ended up on the shoulders of the middle linebacker... in the end zone! "Touchdown," yelled the referee with his arms pointed skyward signaling that I had scored! The partisan crowd went wild! We kicked the extra-point and went ahead 17-7. As we headed for the sidelines I thanked Paul for what he had done and the great Charlie Shaw for his extra effort to enable me to score.

Our defense held Sacramento scoreless for the remainder of the game. Cochran hit Herb Alexander with a 44-yard touchdown pass late in the final moments of the fourth quarter, making the score 24-7 at the final gun. The crowd was cheering. The players were cheering. Everybody connected with the Rhinos was elated as never before. We shook hands with the Statesmen and congratulated them on their fine season and headed towards our locker room. As we passed the crowd in the stands, kids leaning against the rail started asking our players for their chin straps. This was a sign of appreciation that we semi-pro football players had not experienced before. We gladly obliged the kids to the delight of our young fans, and the chagrin of our somewhat miserly owner.

Once in the locker room we indulged in the traditional champagne salute (cheap champagne in our case) shaking the bottles and spraying everyone in sight, drinking some as we did so. We were excited, exhausted, jubilant and fatigued all at once. Steve Corwin and I hugged each other, smiling from ear to ear. I poured champagne over his head and he returned the favor. It was one of the most fantastic experiences of my life and culminated another major step in my quest for a tryout with an NFL team.

On the way to the post-game party, I turned to Kathy and said, "You know, if I would have known that everything would have turned out this way, with such a dramatic ending and scoring a decisive touchdown in the championship game, I would have had all of this filmed... because nobody is going to believe that it really happened."

At the stoplight, Kathy leaned over, gently put her hand on mine, kissed me tenderly on my cheek and said, "I trusted in you all along, and knew in my heart what the outcome would be... because you *believed*."

At our awards dinner a few weeks later I was named Most Inspirational Player by my teammates and coaches. I was honored beyond words. Nearly eleven months after being inspired to undertake a mission to fulfill the responsibility that Coach Crutchfield had instilled in me, here I sat among the group of players and coaches who helped me complete the mission. All the running of lap after lap around the football field, running seemingly endless stadium steps and countless wind sprints were over. Weightlifting, working out running pass patterns at Cal State Long Beach with those great guys who played professional football, all the obstacles and challenges confronted and overcome along the way were now behind me. The tryout for the Rhinos, the practices, traveling and the games played... it was all a life-changing experience; an experience for which I will be forever grateful to God and all those who helped make it happen. Reliving those experiences here today as I type away on my computer still sends chills up and down my spine.

But it gets even better! I had boldly sent a letter to George Allen, then the head coach of the Washington Redskins, to request a tryout. George Allen had been the head football coach for the Los Angeles Rams when I was in high school. As mentioned before, the Rams practiced just across the street from Wilson High School at Blair Field. I admired Coach Allen tremendously because of his work ethic, enthusiasm, knowledge of the game and his ability to get more out of his players than they even knew they had to give. He was a consummate winner and he instilled the drive and the will to win in his teams. As head coach of the Redskins he sometimes took a chance signing older players that other teams thought were washed up, only to have them excel under his leadership. Not only that, but he also took a shot at signing an unknown player, Herb Mulkey, who became the Redskins' kick-return specialist the year they won the NFL Eastern Division Title in 1972. I believed that among all the head coaches in the NFL it would be Allen who would be most likely to give me my shot; a longshot, but a shot. I sent him as many of my press clippings as I could along with my letter and expected a positive reply.

I would not be disappointed. Just a few weeks later I received a letter from George Allen inviting me to attend a free-agent tryout session in Phoenix, Arizona. Yes I can, yes I will, just watch me. I attended that Redskins session in Phoenix, and also one in Salt Lake City, Utah. These sessions were among the most exciting experiences of my life at that point and the final chapter in my improbable mission of 1974. I was amid many free agents from many different parts of the southwest United States who were invited to participate, but no one there could possibly have been as appreciative of this opportunity as I was. This unlikeliest of all free agents, a guy with only one hand trying to compete at running back against some really great athletes; the longest of long shots, but I had been invited and I did my very best to prove myself worthy.

I performed at my highest possible level in drill after drill. It was an honor to be participating in these drills run by Ted Marchibroda, the offensive coordinator for the Redskins at that time who would later become the head football coach for the Baltimore and Indianapolis Colts, as well as the Baltimore Ravens. What a thrill! And I didn't drop any of the balls he threw to me during these drills. Some of the passes that quarterbacks threw went uncaught, but not because I didn't make every effort to catch them. Most of which I did. At the conclusion of the tryouts I did not get signed to a contract nor invited to attend the official pre-season camp for the Redskins. But I had the deep satisfaction of knowing that I had taken my limited athletic ability as far as I possibly could have – farther than most people ever expected or believed possible. I wasn't let down or my spirits diminished in the least, because I had pursued what many believed was an impossible dream, not just an improbable one. It was a mission inspired by Coach Crutchfield and achieved with the help and the support of many, many people along the way. George Allen was responsible for putting this finishing touch to my life-changing experience and for that I will always be tremendously indebted to him.

Major mission accomplished. But, and this is a critical lesson, I soon learned that it was not a destination after all, but just another stop along the incredible journey ahead.

Chapter Twelve

—

Getting Down to Business

"The purpose of life, after all, is to live it, to taste experience to the utmost, to reach out eagerly and without fear for newer and richer experience."

– Eleanor Roosevelt

IT IS REMARKABLE TO LOOK back and remember that after I completed my extraordinary mission, I actually believed that I would never again have to prove myself. That had happened before and I was sadly proven to be quite mistaken. I should have known better by now. I thought I would not have to prove myself to strangers, nor to my peers, my future bosses, my family and friends, nor certainly to myself. After all, hadn't I just showed the world that through hard work, desire, determination, tenacity, preparedness, passion and perseverance I could meet challenges head on and conquer adversity? Who could now possibly doubt my abilities and my resolve? The answer: countless people. People who had never met me, interviewed me, hired me, worked with me or ever heard one syllable uttered about my existence, my athletic achievements, my skills and abilities or frankly, anything else. That's quite a realization for a now 24-year old young man to come to grips with following such a remarkable, life-changing accomplishment.

I now had to refocus on my real career. Leaving behind, but not forgetting, all but the memories and lessons learned during my incredible experiences of the past year; the recognition, accomplishments and the great satisfaction of knowing I had given my very best effort to achieve my goals. It was time to begin working toward re-establishing my reputation for hard work in a vocational context and possessing the determination to succeed at my job or jobs as would be the case over the years to follow.

As we move forward to explore some of the accomplishments in my vocational pursuits that followed the achievement of my seemingly impossible dream, it is critically important to focus on the positive. The recurring theme taken from my successes in athletics and how I exploited the lessons learned in those pursuits to achieve success in my vocational life is what matters most. Rather than moving on in a step-by-step account of my many years of experience in various positions with different companies, some of which were not successes, I have selected a few vignettes that best illustrate how I benefitted from those positive experiences and lessons learned long after playing sports.

Over the next several months I decided that outside lumber sales was not really what I wanted to do for the rest of my life. I was grateful for the experiences that I had while at Sun Lumber Company and especially for being empowered to pursue my goals, but I had a strong desire to enter management. There were no opportunities on the horizon within the wholesale division to do so. I therefore requested and received a transfer from that division into the manager-training program with National Building Centers' (NBC) retail home improvement division. I was assigned to a large retail store in Fullerton.

At first, my reception from the retail folks, many of whom were younger than me, was cool at best. Even Larry Pisoni, an Italian-American who came out of Hell's Kitchen in the Bronx, New York, and his assistant manager, Ed, were less than friendly for a while. They all looked at me as someone who "hadn't paid his dues" by working as a clerk, stock boy or cashier, as they had, yet I was placed in a management trainee position. I could empathize with them, but didn't feel particularly guilty.

Over time I was able to win nearly all of them over. What sealed the deal and made me truly "one of them," was when we remodeled the entire store. I was right in there helping all of them with all the dirty work involved, and when I was high up on ladders helping to repaint the walls, "Bingo," I was in. When I was painting, the corporation's CEO was visiting our store and he almost had me pulled from the ladders because of, you guessed it, the "liability." By this time Larry and I were buddies and he assured the CEO that I was doing a great job and not to worry about me. I continued painting.

Within ten months of joining the retail division I was promoted and given the opportunity to manage another one of NBC's retail home improvement centers not far from Fullerton in the City of Orange. The first thing I did was remodel the store, staying well into the early morning hours of the next day for over a week painting walls, moving gondolas and helping our crew to make the changes I felt the store needed to be more customer friendly and enhance sales. We also moved out left-over stock of everything from nails, bolts and screws to brackets, paint and assorted hardware that had been buried for years in nooks and crannies no one apparently had ever checked.

Although my store's sales numbers had risen dramatically and I had greatly enhanced morale, over the next several months I became unhappy being in retail and having to work crazy hours and all holidays and weekends. I had young children and wasn't getting to spend much time with them. I began pursuing other interests and resigned to look for another career opportunity. It would have been wiser to find that opportunity *before* resigning, of course. Boy was Kathy ever happy with me… *not!* I was now unemployed with a wife and two children. Luckily, Kathy was working as a telephone operator at a local hospital. In just a couple of weeks, however, my fortunes changed for the better.

In 1976 Dad was again working for Nathan Shapell, this time as the President of Shapell of San Diego, a division within Shapell Industries which built homes and condominiums in San Diego County. Nepotism is generally referred to in the negative at most companies, but Nathan Shapell encouraged it within his. He had several cousins and other relatives working within his firm, including his only son, Bobby and his son-in-law, Paul Guerin. He also encouraged others within the company who were not related to him to bring members of their families into the fold. This was born out of the fact that Nathan and David Shapell, as well as their wives and sister who married their partner, Max Webb, were all Jewish Holocaust survivors. They cherished family first. With my situation in mind, Dad approached Nathan with the possibility of my joining S&S Construction Company; the home-building subsidiary of Shapell Industries, Inc. Nathan had told Dad to think about bringing his sons into his business in the past, so he suggested that I go to work as an assistant purchasing agent in the corporate headquarters in Beverly Hills, reporting to one of his long-time purchasing agents, a lady who shall forever remain nameless.

It didn't take me long to figure out that the "lady" for whom I was now an assistant was not to be fooled with.

She had a deep enough voice that on more than one occasion I overheard her on the telephone remarking to the caller, "I am not a sir!" And her demeanor matched her coarse voice. I saw her numerous times red-line a report or contract draft that had been typed (pre-PC, of course) by her administrative assistant that now had to be completely retyped. She ranted and raved on a regular basis. She also expected me to serve her and her guests coffee and several times even asked me to pick up her laundry. I was determined to extricate myself from this position, which I did by explaining to Mr. Shapell that I also wanted to work for other purchasing agents to get a feel for how others functioned in this position. Thankfully, he agreed with the idea.

After several more months away from the monster purchasing agent, even though things were going much better since my liberation, I was looking for a way to move up in the company so that I could earn more money and advance my career. I wasn't sure how I was going to accomplish that, but I consciously started thinking of ways to do so. I thought back to how I succeeded in accomplishing other goals in my life, particularly with respect to my life-changing experience playing football for the Rhinos just two years prior. I asked myself, "What were the things I did to make that happen?" As they came to me I wrote them down:

- Be bold - set goals and have a plan,
- Develop a burning desire and a passion to achieve your goal,
- Be willing to work hard and sacrifice,
- Be flexible and embrace change, and
- Be determined to overcome adversity to succeed.

I believed that these elements, which I applied when I embarked on my "impossible" dream, were exactly what I now needed to apply in order for me to move forward... and *up* at Shapell Industries. However, I needed a specific goal on which to focus.

One day soon after writing down the bullet points above, which I later referred to as my "Golden Rules – The Winning Ways to Peak Performance," I came upon an article in *Builder* magazine discussing the entrance of some of Shapell's competitors into the arena of "affordable housing." These were new home products that were farther out in the suburbs built on cheaper land and less expensive than the top-of-the-line housing developments we were building. These homes were mostly targeted to first-time buyers, like me. I certainly couldn't afford a Shapell home on my salary.

I began to see the opening of a window of opportunity. I then took the initiative to write a memo to Nathan asking why we as a leader in the homebuilding industry in California weren't also in this more affordable housing market; after all, we were one of the most successful new home development companies in the country. I had no idea what his reaction or response would be to my memo, but it was a part of a master plan of building on my initiative to achieve my goal of upward mobility. I sent it to him anyway.

A couple of days after sending the memo, Nathan asked to see me. He was intrigued by what I had written, but asked, "Young man, what makes you think we can build this type of product?" I replied to him that I didn't know for sure, but simply felt that if those other builders could, why couldn't we?

Nathan then surprised me by telling me that I had two weeks to go out and do a "market survey" and come back with my findings and recommendations. He said to drop everything else that I was working on to concentrate on this special assignment. I said, "Yes, sir, Mr. Shapell!" I then got up and left his office, determined to do my level best on this market survey. Only one problem; I had no clue as to what all was entailed in preparing a market survey. Undeterred I asked Dad how I should go about preparing my report to Nathan. He told me to go to as many affordable home projects as I could throughout Southern California.

"Ask the salespeople questions, study the floor plans, exterior design and building materials used and gather as much information as you can to analyze the potential for Shapell Industries to build and sell such a product, profitably," Dad said. "Then simply write a report about what you have learned."

I don't remember how many new home communities I visited or how many salespeople I spoke with, but it was a significant number. At first these sales people were reluctant to offer up any information. I discovered that when they had tried to elicit information from S&S salespeople they could get almost no cooperation at all. It took some doing, but I eventually was able to get them to be more open to my "gentle persuasion." I learned far more than they probably ever dreamed of revealing to anyone in my position. For whatever reason I was able to make them feel comfortable doing so. In addition to the important information I was there to retrieve, I also learned more about their personal lives than I ever thought necessary.

I recorded the average square footage of their models, what types of building materials were used inside and out, especially in the kitchens and bathrooms, how many bedrooms and baths each model contained, how many units were being built and in how many phases, etc. I also recorded the average sales prices and what the surrounding areas were like; what were the community amenities and was there a homeowners association? I reported on as much information as I could and compared this data with the products we built. As I neared the deadline I had a bit of a dilemma, because I had not yet learned how to type. I was either going to have to teach myself real quickly how to do so or hand-write the entire report. I decided to hand-write the report because I felt it would set my report apart from any others Nathan had no doubt ever received. I also was being realistic, since learning to type was going to be too time consuming at this juncture. That would have to wait.

My penmanship had always been above average, especially my printing, so I decided to print my report longhand using colored felt-tipped Flair pens to give it some character. My style of writing then as now is to tell a story as if I were talking directly to the reader, often interspersing humor and anecdotal information. I wanted my report to be as interesting as one can make such a thing. When I had finished the report I decided to draw an illustration on the cover that reflected the contents of my report, much like a political cartoon tells a vivid story in one or two frames. I thought that either Nathan would appreciate my sense of humor and special touch, or he'd think he'd made a mistake giving me such an important assignment. Be bold, I always say, and this was no different.

My conclusion, in my view, clearly made the case for why Shapell Industries *should* have been building more affordable homes in addition to the upscale communities for which we were well known. It was a fairly lengthy report and I had worked very hard to gather the information, analyze it and put into writing my findings well into the early morning hours for several days preparing it; not only because of the length of material but especially because I sometimes made errors in spelling or needed to change things around. That's a real problem when you hand-write a report! Many pages had to be completely re-written. Anyway, I turned in my report on time and awaited Nathan's response. I didn't have to wait long.

I had turned in the report to Nathan on a Friday. He called me into his office the following Monday morning.

"Young man," he began. "While I don't agree with everything I read in your wonderful report, I want you to work in our marketing department and do market surveys on a regular basis in Orange County and the Inland Empire. And I'm giving you a raise."

You could have heard a pin drop. I was being promoted on the spot by the Chairman of the Board. Nathan went on to say that he wanted me to no longer work in the purchasing department. He now wanted me to report to the marketing director. Once again my plan had worked. Some people might call this "luck." Sure, it's luck; but luck, as I have already mentioned, is when preparedness meets opportunity. I thanked Nathan and called Kathy. She was quite pleased, and so was I, for I had achieved another important goal on my own initiative, hard work and determination to succeed.

In just a few short months I was promoted again, to Director of Market Research for S&S Construction Company. I traveled throughout the state gathering information and preparing market survey reports for Nathan and the senior managers. I received considerable praise from Nathan and other executive and senior managers at the company for my reports. As an example, I received the following note from Nathan Shapell on April 13, 1977:

"It was so lonely here last night until I found you in that little corner working away and realized that I was not the only person in the world still awake.

Now, may I tell you that as impressed as I have been time after time to receive your marketing reports, impressed both with the creativity and wit and with the content, you have really exceeded my expectations with this latest one. It is simply the greatest I have ever seen and it is a pleasure to show other people so they can share my pride.

You are really something else, Lynn, and even though I have told you many times how proud all of us, and especially I, are of you, permit me to say it again. You are doing an outstanding job and making a real contribution to this company. And as much as we do recognize it now, I have a feeling that as time goes by, we will appreciate it even more.

Please continue your great work and accept again my gratitude for your attitude, your dedication and the results.

–Nathan

This was only one such note I received from Mr. Shapell, but it was certainly one of my favorite. He was a great man, and like Frank Higgins and Coach Crutchfield, he took a personal interest in me. He had confidence in me and encouraged me to always do my very best. Nathan received maximum effort from me because he seemed so sincere when offering me praise of any sort. He was one of the greatest men I have ever known.

In late 1978 I had grown a bit restless just doing the marketing survey reports and wanted to have even more responsibility within the company. I don't know why I tend to get dissatisfied with the status quo and continually seek new challenges and opportunities, even when things are going well, but I always have. I am not an analyst of that sort. I have never sought the answer or answers to that dilemma. I just know that I am who I am. I decided to set my sights on a new goal; I wanted to work in the advertising department at Shapell Industries. I had always been creative and somewhat artistic, but had no formal education in advertising or public relations. No matter, I didn't have any formal education in market research either, but I became the director of market research for a major new home developer anyway;

and did quite well. Advertising was a discipline I was simply drawn to after working so closely with our marketing director. All I needed was another window of opportunity to make this new goal a reality.

Then, one Monday morning I was sitting in on a marketing meeting as was customary to review the sales activity at all of our new home communities over the past weekend and also discuss the effectiveness of our print advertisements in the local newspapers. On this particular morning Nathan was upset because one of our newspaper ads had received particularly bad reviews from members of the board of directors, the sales manager, many of our sales people and others. The current advertising director was generally on the hot seat. Although he was a veteran ad man he didn't have good instincts relative to our company, or how to create ads which were both effective and that pleased Nathan. He was beat up badly at this meeting.

That morning I developed another bold plan and set another targeted goal; I was going to take the initiative and redesign the ad that caused the uproar at the meeting. I would then indicate to Nathan that I had a strong interest in working in the advertising department. Just to plant a seed for another move upward; ultimately, however, to become the Director of Advertising and Public Relations for Shapell Industries. I knew it might take a while. This was another longshot, but I would prepare myself now for an eventual opening.

I cut up the ad in question, but didn't rewrite copy; I simply laid out the new ad using the same elements but arranged them in a more desirable layout. I used common sense more than anything else. Then I immediately walked down to Nathan's office, got an audience with him, showed him my ad and told him that if given the chance, I could be his next advertising director. He told me I was more valuable to the company in other ways and that advertising people could be "bought," so to speak, anywhere. He was implying that he held little respect for them. Undeterred once again I stressed that this was something I had a strong interest in pursuing.

I only wanted to use this opportunity to plant a seed, nothing more. How was I to know that Nathan was going to take my new ad to the advertising director and throw it on his desk saying, "If Lynn Effinger can do this right, why can't you?" But that's exactly what he did. Not part of my plan, I assure you.

About a week later I was called into the advertising director's office. He explained to me that he was made aware that I had an interest in getting involved with the advertising and public relations activities of the company and he wanted me to become his assistant. I was on my way to potentially achieving another important goal.

I began learning the basics of the advertising process and the development of press releases under the ad man's direction. Press releases contain information about our company, people, products and events disseminated to newspapers and trade publications that might be newsworthy enough to be developed into news stories to appear in these vehicles. There were also some special projects that I was assigned. This included coming up with a new look for our company logo, which I proudly did with the assistance of a talented, ultra-creative outside design studio.

About two months later, after successfully training in the department under the battered ad director and completing the projects to which I had been assigned, he abruptly resigned. I was now the only person in the entire company who knew anything about what was going on with our advertising and public relations programs. I decided to strike while the proverbial iron was still hot. I immediately went to Nathan to again let him know how much I wanted to be his next director of advertising and public relations. I told him about the things I had already learned and that I was confident that I could do the kind of job he expected and deserved. My desire to win this promotion had grown exponentially overnight because I could literally visualize myself in this high-profile position and doing well. Mr. Shapell took in what I had to say and then said he was going to start looking for a replacement immediately. I could work for the new person for a year or two, and if I was still interested in the position after that timeframe we could revisit the subject. That was not good enough for me to a point. I think he was under the impression that I would drop the idea over time. Wrong. I moved ahead as the interim ad director until such time as the new person was hired.

It became rather obvious after a while that either Nathan didn't like the candidates he interviewed or the candidates didn't like Nathan or the offer to join our company. For whatever reason, no one had been hired two full months following the resignation of my predecessor. In the meantime, I had teamed up with our outside advertising designer and we created some impressive brochures for our newest townhouse communities. We also standardized all of our ad formats with a special border treatment and placement of our new logo. It was instantly recognized by the reader that these specific ads were touting the quality, luxury and style of homes built by S&S Construction Company. No matter where they appeared. I had also standardized our brochure covers and onsite and offsite signage for most of our single-family developments. This helped the company economize on advertising expenditures since we had nearly twenty communities either under construction, for sale, or in the planning stages at any given time.

I then made another significant decision; my designer and I would put together a presentation demonstrating what we had already accomplished in just two months and what we had planned moving forward. It was quite an impressive show that we presented to Nathan and all the other senior managers. It was exciting enough that upon the conclusion of the presentation Nathan called me into his office where he said to me, "Young man, you are now the Director of Advertising and Public Relations for Shapell Industries and S&S Construction Company." And with that he gave me a large bonus on the spot; amazing.

For a little more than a year I served in this exciting position. It was one of the most fun experiences I have ever had in a job. I was able to express myself creatively while being in a key position at the heart of our great company. Under the age of 30, I was responsible for all advertising and public relations activities for one of the largest, most successful new homebuilding companies in America.

Having started with the firm essentially as a "gopher" for a purchasing agent, this was quite an achievement in just over three years with the company.

In late 1979, two events took place that impacted my life forever; Kathy gave birth to our third child, Christopher Thomas Effinger on October 22nd. Chris was a true gift from God. Kathy and I had not expected to have another child since we already had a boy and a girl. However, she had come down with some health issues and her doctor recommended that she stop taking her birth-control pills. Just for a while. Boom! Very shortly thereafter she became pregnant. Right from the very start our unexpected third child became a wonderful, happy baby boy who later grew into a sweet, loving child. Chris was also easy to raise throughout his teenage years, which was greatly appreciated, since not all parents are as fortunate. He has matured into a fine young man who is now a loving husband and father. Chris has become over the years a close friend and confidant in addition to being our son.

The second event was that I again started looking for a bigger challenge beyond working as an employee. I had an entrepreneurial streak that I no doubt inherited from Dad. I decided that because I had come to enjoy advertising so much and created and produced so many quality ads and other materials for Shapell with ease that I believed I could provide similar services to other home builders as a consultant. This was certainly a bold belief, never before having been in business for myself. The more I thought about it the more excited I became. I was committed to establishing Effinger & Associates, a marketing communications consulting firm specializing in the new home development industry, as soon as possible.

Telling Nathan that I was going to leave the company after all he had done for me was very difficult. My plan had been to resign in October of 1979 so that I didn't hang around as a lame duck until year end just so that I could collect my yearly bonus check. He made it more difficult when he said that I shouldn't be stupid and told me to stay until December 31st. I said to him, "That wouldn't be fair." But he shook his head and replied, "Life isn't fair, young man, do as I ask." I did, receiving a large bonus check despite having announced my pending resignation just before Christmas. While I was very excited to now be going out on my own, I did not foresee the difficult struggles that awaited me.

Chapter Thirteen

A Roller Coaster Existence

"It is not the critic who counts: not the man who points out how the strong man stumbles or where the doer of deeds could have done better; The credit belongs to the man who is actually in the arena, whose face is marred by dust and sweat and blood, who strives valiantly, who errs and comes up short again and again, because he knows the great enthusiasms, the great devotions, who spends himself for a worthy cause; who, at the best, knows, in the end, the triumph of high achievement, and who, at the worst, if he fails, at least he fails while daring greatly, so that his place shall never be with those cold and timid souls who know neither victory nor defeat."

– Theodore Roosevelt

The phrase, "Timing is everything," might not be 100 percent accurate, but it sure applied to my decision to become a consultant, and not in a good way. Securing homebuilder clients in 1980 was not as difficult as getting paid to provide them with marketing communications services. Times were tough and home sales declined sharply. Interest rates rose so quickly that many potential home buyers could no longer qualify for a loan. The term "creative financing" suddenly came into play as a necessity to sell homes. Advertising agencies do not build homes. Therefore they are typically among the last vendors to be paid by developers in difficult times. Sometimes they don't get paid at all. That was true for this marketing consultant, as well.

I continued to struggle throughout 1980 and in the months and years that followed. There were months at a time when I was unemployed. We eventually had to sell the first home we had ever owned together to avoid foreclosure, which did not help my relationship with Kathy at that time. As someone who came from what was considered a traditional household where the father always provided for the family, I assure you that I felt no small amount of guilt. My oldest son is still upset with me for allowing the situation to change so dramatically for the family by making a regrettable career decision that could have been avoided. The knowledge that Nathan had tried to dissuade me from leaving his company made it worse. My confidence in my abilities and belief in myself were at an all-time low. I took whatever work in advertising I could find and struggled for the next couple of years to get my career back on track.

Over the next several years I continued working off and on as a marketing consultant to home builders and developers. I also served as a marketing director for a manufacturing company, a sales rep for an advertising design studio, creative director for an advertising agency, sales rep for a newspaper publishing company and for nearly two years I was the publisher and editor of *Escondido* magazine. All of these jobs were taken in reaction to events, rather than through careful goal setting, and proactive business planning. The cumulative experiences were valuable, but without direction or planning they were just jobs; a way to bring home some income. Reaction is no way to succeed, quite to the contrary it is a prescription for failure.

But failure is not the end of the world. It is painful, but we can and do learn from failure. I subscribe to the sentiment expressed so profoundly in a speech by Theodore Roosevelt about the "man in the arena." While I don't want to minimize the struggles from the time I went out on my own in 1980 until 1987, there is nothing significant to reveal to you about those lean, mean years. Suffice it to know that no great goals were set, and no extraordinary effort was made to proactively rise above my circumstances. It was as though I had already forgotten the lessons I had learned in achieving success in sports and while employed by Nathan. I believe it is more beneficial for you to learn more about the successes that followed these tough years. Years that added to my life experiences and helped me grow stronger in the long run despite the struggles.

Our children in 1984 (L to R) Scott, Diana and Christopher.

In 1987 I was hired to become the marketing director for The Jelley Company, real estate brokerage in Del Mar, California. Joe Jelley (yes, that's his real name), was a tough, driven entrepreneur who operated several up-scale real estate offices on the west coast in San Diego County.

Having a full-time position once again was a refreshing change. It was nice knowing how much take home pay I would have every two weeks and the job offered moderate health care benefits. My main responsibilities included attending the weekly sales meetings in both our Del Mar and La Jolla offices, writing and placing dozens of three-line or four-line classified ads for available properties, creating display advertisements and writing and distributing news releases. I also helped the real estate agents with sales fliers and any brochures or other collateral materials they needed. It wasn't the most taxing job I'd ever had, but it was a decent one in a beautiful coastal environment. I made quite a few friends within the company, which boasted five offices and was continuing to expand to other locations.

One of the other things I did was to occasionally coordinate seminars for our agents, sometimes leading the sessions myself. The first such seminar where I was a presenter was titled, "The Secret to Success in Real Estate." It was the most heavily attended seminar the company had ever held. Many real estate agents are constantly on the hunt for a magic bullet or secret plan that will make listing and selling real estate easier, providing higher and higher commissions. They spend untold sums of money going to seminars, conferences and other meetings in search of the "secret" to success. Knowing this I decided to attract them to attend my session like mosquitoes to a light bulb by titling my presentation the way I did. The "catch" was that in the first sentence of my presentation I told them that there was no "secret" to success in real estate – Success is attained in real estate just like in every other endeavor; through appropriate planning and goal-setting, hard work and tenacity. I stressed that there is no substitute for hard work. The agents were not amused; at first, anyway. But I did provide them with sound marketing advice and other information that would help them to be better, stronger real estate professionals. Joe Jelley was impressed with how I handled this seminar and that I focused on assuring his agents that they should stop tilting at windmills in search of the elusive secret to success.

After about 18 months on the job at The Jelley Company I once again felt I was underutilizing my skills and abilities. I certainly wasn't making enough money commensurate with same, at least in my opinion. One of the things that boosted my confidence back to earlier levels was an opportunity I had to play tennis in a March of Dimes charity doubles tournament run by Rolf Benirshke, the popular place kicker for the San Diego Chargers at the time. Quite a bit of publicity was generated by my participation in the tournament, which also highlighted my previous achievements in football. This served to remind *me* that I knew full well how to be successful when I put my mind to it and made the necessary effort to do so. I played very well throughout the tournament where we were paired with professional tennis players and finished among the top ten entrants among several dozen players. Competition is healthy. It rekindled my faith in my abilities and I regained my self-confidence. Success in one area of endeavor begets success in another. The opposite is also quite true. I discovered that reality during the tough years from 1980 to 1987.

One of Jelley's location managers had recently left the company to open his own independent real estate office in Solana Beach with a partner, just a few miles from Jelley's headquarters. He asked me to help him with all of their marketing materials and weekly ads for Silver Pacific Real Estate. I did so for several weeks until Joe Jelley discovered that I was freelancing for another real estate brokerage.

He told me in no uncertain terms that I could not have two masters. As I mentioned earlier, Joe Jelley was a tough son-of-a-gun who was an authoritarian by nature. I decided that I would rather work with the other gentleman and also look for other real estate brokerages that I could represent on a consulting basis. Jelley told me I was making a big mistake, but with new confidence in my abilities I chose to leave. I worked with Silver Pacific and picked up another client in Vista, California, Realty World-Dale Wood. Things were progressing nicely.

At a Board of Realtors fundraising event several months after being hired on a consulting basis by the Realty World franchise I met Don Stafford. He was the general manager of Century 21 Ambassador Realty in Oceanside. He told me he was impressed with the number of news releases I was getting published for the Realty World franchise. He also said that his office was expanding and he'd be interested in talking to me about becoming their marketing director on a consulting basis. Don and I got together at his office a couple of days later. He offered to hire me and pay me what I considered to be a very fair consulting fee. I was flattered and didn't take very long to decide that I would accept his offer. The only catch was that I would have to give up my assignment with the Realty World franchise because these two companies were in direct competition with one another. Because of the potential offered at Century 21 Ambassador, and the increased income I would derive, I felt the wise decision was to part with Realty World.

Working with both Silver Pacific Real Estate and Century 21 Ambassador proved over time to be a difficult task. After a little more than a year in business the partners at Silver Pacific were struggling to succeed which meant they had cash flow issues. I gave that assignment up.

One day in early 1989 I received a call from the director of public relations for Century 21 International. He said that a clipping service sent him hundreds of press clippings from newspapers each week that were generated by all the Century 21 franchises across the country. He was giving a seminar at the upcoming Century 21 International Convention in Dallas, Texas in a month or so and when he saw that I was generating far more press clippings for Century 21 Ambassador than all of the other 90 San Diego-area Century 21 franchises combined, he knew he needed to talk to me. After explaining my background and my process to him he invited me to come to Dallas and participate in his session to help other franchisees learn how to generate press coverage. Such PR efforts are essentially free to those companies who submit news releases as opposed to paying for ad space exclusively. As long as there is someone in your real estate brokerage who will generate these releases. Otherwise there is a small fee for someone like myself to generate them. Even then the cost is minimal compared to the cost of advertising space.

Century 21 Ambassador paid my way to participate and it was a great experience. I addressed a near capacity breakout session and explained how it was that I was so prolific at writing and submitting press releases and instructed them how to replicate the success I enjoyed in their own franchises.

Each time I gave a live presentation I would weave in some of my motivational presentation. I felt it was my duty to do so in order to continue fulfilling my responsibility, as articulated earlier. The more I did so, the more I sought other opportunities to speak before an audience; anytime, anywhere.

While I was serving as the marketing director for Century 21 Ambassador I decided that I wanted to have a weekly radio talk show to promote the company and their agents. It would also enable me to generate additional clients and hopefully, more income. The idea had come to me because I had interviewed a friend of mine, George Chamberlin at his radio studio to do a feature article on him for the local newspaper. George was in the stockbrokerage business but also did a daily morning talk show, *Money Matters*. He and I played tennis together with other guys in doubles matches nearly every Saturday and Sunday morning for years.

While I was taking pictures of George behind the microphone during one of his programs, it suddenly occurred to me that I could do this, too. Why not? So I talked with the station manager, told him my concept for a weekly radio talk show called, creatively enough, *Real Estate Matters*. He liked the idea and said all I had to do was buy air time and then sell commercial time to cover that expense, which I did. *Real Estate Matters* was born! It was one of the most fun activities I ever participated in. I produced each show, wrote most of the commercials and did voice-overs on many of them. I was, of course, the host each week. I did the show for about 18 months, but other opportunities that came along later ended my run sooner than I would have liked. But it was a terrific experience. I thought about doing a cable television program as well, but decided that I had a face that was perfect for radio.

As for George, who was a big help to me in the beginning of doing the show, he continues doing his weekday radio show, serves as a financial reporter and analyst on the NBC-TV affiliate station in San Diego, and is the Executive Editor of the *San Diego Daily Transcript*. He is a good friend of mine and my older brother.

Kathy had earned her real estate license in 1988. Although she continued to serve as customer service manager for a successful company in San Diego she decided to sell real estate as well. By late 1989 she had become the top-producing agent in her real estate office in Escondido, even though she was a part-time agent! The company she chose to work for was Great Western Real Estate, a subsidiary of Great Western Financial, the parent company of Great Western Bank. Great Western Financial in the late '80s had purchased Walker & Lee Real Estate, a well-known and respected real estate company with offices throughout the State of California. It had been their belief that by owning a real estate company Great Western Bank would generate significantly more home loans from their Realtor network. They renamed the company, Great Western Real Estate.

In early 1990 the manager at Kathy's real estate office had mentioned to her that Great Western Real Estate's director of advertising and public relations had been terminated for letting advertising expenditures escalate far above her allotted budget. Kathy's manager knew I had successfully represented several real estate-related clients and liked my work, so she encouraged Kathy to have me call Great Western Real Estate's chief operating officer, John Haltom, to arrange an interview for this open position. I was not interested, but after being prodded several times I called John Haltom, who interviewed me via telephone before inviting me to meet with him in person the following week.

Because I was not particularly interested in changing what I was doing and didn't feel any pressure whatsoever in my face-to-face interview with John, I probably had the best interview of my career. John asked me what it would take for me to accept the position. Not particularly wanting to accept it, I blurted out a salary figure that I thought was quite high. John said, "We could do that." I suddenly became interested in the position after all. I was hired by John Haltom to become the Director of Advertising and Public Relations for Great Western Real Estate just a couple of weeks after my interview. I had to give up most of my consulting clients in order to accept the position, which I was reluctant to do, but could not continue to serve them all well while working full time for Great Western. This was the best career move I had made since joining Shapell in 1976 and the highest salary I had ever been paid up to that point. I was excited to be going to work for such a distinguished organization and was about to embark on another significant part of my life's journey.

In 1988 and 1989 the real estate market across the country and in California in particular, went through the roof. It was not unusual for listing agents to receive multiple offers on properties higher than the listing price. It was a "feeding frenzy" that made it a seller's market, one of many such events that happen just about every decade. It was in this environment that Great Western Financial had purchased Walker & Lee. Unfortunately, by the middle of 1990 the market had changed. The demand for real estate began to decline, as did property values. Interest rates on mortgages were again near ten percent which added to this decline in sales, as did world tensions caused by actions of Saddam Hussein in Iraq.

While the early months of my employment at Great Western Real Estate had been productive and rewarding, it was becoming apparent as the year progressed that the company was having financial difficulties. And so were many of our real estate agents, many of whom had been top-producers in the late '80s but had not sold a single house in 1990. The real estate market had plummeted and things looked bleak on the horizon. My assessment was that there had been far too many high-priced managers within the organization sucking the life-blood out of operating expenses. This, as much as economic conditions, did them in. As did the fact that Great Western Bank wasn't capturing anywhere near the percentage of loans they had hoped for when they purchased Walker & Lee. Realtors send their clients to the lenders they feel will give them the best loan, no matter where their paychecks are derived.

On another sunny, but windy Monday morning in November of 1990 all of the managers and support personnel at Great Western Real Estate's headquarters were ushered into the training room. Security guards locked the entry and exit doors behind us. Rather unusual, but telling. The President of Great Western Real Estate, Bob McNitt, proceeded to inform us that Great Western Financial had made the decision to cease operations of the real estate subsidiary and close most of the 35 offices we operated throughout the state. They had decided to sell the two successful offices in the greater Palm Springs area to an independent chain of real estate offices. Another office or two were to be sold to former employees of Great Western; so much for my career at Great Western Real Estate. While most of the managers and employees were let go immediately, I was one of the managers that John Haltom had asked to stay on to help dissolve the company. I had no other immediate prospects, so I decided to help during this transition.

In early January of 1991 I decided to start looking for clients again for whom I could begin providing marketing communications services. I formulated a plan that included leveraging my relationships with Great Western Real Estate agents who would soon be joining other real estate companies for whom I could possibly provide public relations services on a consulting basis as they joined other real estate offices. I would be on my own once again. Not essentially a bold plan this time, and another somewhat risky one that was born out of necessity. I was reacting, but seemed to have somewhat brighter prospects now that I had substantially improved my resume.

Some of the real estate agents in our GWRE Scripps Ranch office had transferred over to ERA The Property Store, a successful real estate franchise owned by two partners. Our agents had asked the broker at the ERA franchise if I could write press releases for them announcing their move. These nice people were very complimentary about me to the broker. He not only agreed that I could write the releases in question, he asked me to come meet with him to discuss doing press releases for his entire staff of salespeople. This gentleman, Rick Hoffman, was also the president of the San Diego County ERA Brokers Council, made up of the owners of all 25 ERA franchises in the county. Rick told me that if I did a good job for his office he would allow me to pitch the other brokers in the group at one of their monthly meetings. We agreed on a monthly consulting fee and I began representing his company that day. He also invited Kathy and me to attend the upcoming San Diego County ERA Awards Dinner. I informed John Haltom that it was time for me to move on. He thanked me for my service and I returned to consulting.

On January 17, 1991 coalition air forces commenced bombardment of Iraqi military positions. Saddam Hussein had invaded Kuwait and brutalized the citizenry six months earlier. The United States Military and a worldwide coalition of armed forces attacked Iraq and ultimately drove the Iraqi Army out of Kuwait, liberating that country from Hussein's brutality. Operation Desert Storm was a magnificent operation that ultimately lasted just over a month, culminating in a ground assault that succeeded in defeating the Iraqi Army in just 100 hours.

Attendees at the ERA Awards Dinner on January 17th were on edge that evening after many of us had watched on CNN as the war commenced in living color and in real time. It didn't help our nerves when an ice sculpture crashed to the floor because a spotlight had been pointed at its base. We were further unnerved when an indoor fireworks show went off. Not a figurative fireworks show. A real fireworks show complete with explosions, sparkling fire and smoke! "Who was the moron who decided to go through with that tonight of all nights," I wondered... out loud.

In no time my performance on behalf of ERA The Property Store led not only to my being hired by the San Diego County Brokers Council, I was subsequently hired to provide public relations services to the ERA Brokers Councils in Los Angeles County, Orange County, the Inland Empire, and Ventura County. In addition, several of the larger franchisees from each county hired me for their individual offices. I represented over 100 ERA franchises throughout Southern California, in less than three months after leaving Great Western Real Estate.

For the next year I was busier than a one-armed paper hanger (sorry, I couldn't resist). And I was making a decent living to boot. The real estate market continued to tank, however. Foreclosures were on the rise across the country, spreading into California behind the rest of the U.S., but finally hitting us hard in 1992. As a result, throughout 1992 many real estate companies were struggling to stay open. Many did not, including several ERA franchises. I began losing accounts not because of performance issues, but because offices cut their marketing budgets or were going out of business. I still had a few clients, which kept me going while looking for other potential business opportunities, but our financial situation at home was quickly deteriorating once again.

Chapter Fourteen

The Journey Continues

"If what you did yesterday seems big, you haven't done anything today."

– Lou Holtz

The Journey Continues

ON NOVEMBER 30, 1992 GOD brought Holly Louise Maeva into our family. Our daughter, Diana, had gotten married earlier that year and now had given birth to her first and subsequently only child. Kathy was only 40 years old and I had just turned 42 three weeks earlier, but to say we were proud to be grandparents is beyond an understatement. Holly occupies a very special place in my heart. We are tremendously close, and I love her dearly. I am so grateful that she came into our lives when she did.

It's hard to believe, but Holly graduated from high school in May of 2011 and will be going off to college this fall. She has matured into a beautiful, intelligent young lady who has a bright future in the medical profession ahead of her. She was in the AVID program at her high school for four years and earned acceptance to a major university. This was due to her scholastic efforts, but also because of the guidance and unbelievable support she received from her AVID counselor. We are tremendously proud of Holly.

When things aren't going the way I want them to or there are outside pressures weighing heavily upon my shoulders for whatever reason, a gentle kiss on the cheek, a hug or an, "I love you, Papa," from my Holly makes life good again.

Our precious Holly at four years old
(Photograph by Carolyn Abacherli)

In early 1993 I was sitting in my home office working on ERA press releases when the telephone suddenly started to ring. On the line was my former boss when I served as Director of Advertising and Public Relations for Great Western Real Estate.

"Hey Lynn, how's it going," drawled John Haltom in his best Texas accent. "I'm guessing you're not making a million dollars a year yet, so how would you like to work for me again?"

He was correct of course. No million bucks here. John had stayed with the real estate subsidiary long enough to completely close down the operation for Great Western Financial. He then had been asked to join the management team at Great Western Bank in their mortgage loan default servicing division as REO (real estate owned) manager. REOs are residential real estate properties that the bank owns after foreclosing on delinquent loans. The banks are in the lending business and don't want these non-performing real estate assets on their books because they negatively impact their balance sheets. They dispose of the properties by listing them with local real estate agents. John said Great Western had over 3,000 REOs in their inventory at that point and were, unfortunately, acquiring over 400 more each month through foreclosure.

I think it is quite important to add here that some people might think that working for a bank to sell the homes they have foreclosed on is making money at the expense of others' misfortune. On the contrary, many of these loans were taken out by investors. Some were slum lords. It is truly unfortunate that for a variety of reasons people are no longer able or willing to make their mortgage payments. And I do have empathy for these people. But the fact is that I am a real estate marketing expert and problem solver. I was honored to be approached to help the bank solve their REO problem knowing that my number one objective was to work myself out of a job. If I did so it would mean the bank would no longer have such a serious problem and we would be doing our part to help the economy recover. This was as true back in 1993 as it is today.

John also said he had tremendous respect for my marketing abilities and common sense and wanted to know if I would be interested in becoming a marketing consultant to him and the REO department at the bank. In all honesty, all I knew about REO then was how to spell it. I knew they were foreclosed properties, but I didn't know the mechanics of foreclosures or the processes involved in managing, marketing and disposing of them. But I was interested because at that point it looked like if you wanted to remain active in the housing business but weren't involved in foreclosures you better get involved, and quickly. He invited me to Great Western Bank's new headquarters in Chatsworth, California in the heart of the San Fernando Valley to discuss his needs and what he thought I could do to help him with the bank's growing foreclosure problem.

At our lunch meeting, John explained that he was interested in exploring new marketing strategies for helping to flush out more of these residential properties. He was principally focused on the higher-end properties, which at that time were in the $500,000 and up price range. One of the things that impressed me right off the bat was that GWB's REO department refurbished about 90 percent of all REOs. This was done in order to protect neighborhoods from decreasing values to the extent possible. That was good for these communities but also made good business sense for GWB since they continued to make loans in these neighborhoods.

After giving me a high-level overview of the entire foreclosure and REO processes John asked me what it would take to entice me to sign on as a marketing consultant. I told him I'd like to think about it and get back to him, which he said was fine. I wanted to make sure I didn't give my services away, but didn't want to price myself out of this opportunity either. I did tell him that I wasn't prepared to give up the ERA clients that I still served. He was okay with that, which I thought was a good sign.

After seeking advice from Kathy and then my dad I came up with a figure and contacted John by phone. I gave him a range and he said, "We can do that," and indicated that he could approve the high-end of the range I had given him. That was music to my ears. I soon was hired through a one-year consulting contract.

Fortunately, GWB had a satellite REO office in Scripps Ranch just down the street from ERA The Property Store. That meant I only had to go to the Chatsworth headquarters on an as-needed basis and once per month for sales meetings. It was 110 miles from the home we bought in Menifee when I worked for Great Western Real Estate to GWB's headquarters, and only 65 miles each way to Scripps Ranch.

It didn't take me long to discover that this was an exciting opportunity. An opportunity to not only work for such a distinguished corporate giant, but also an opportunity to learn the REO business, which was on the rise due to mounting bad economic conditions. I looked around at the more than 100 employees working in the REO department and said to myself, boldly, "I could run this operation someday," and soon developed a plan to achieve that goal. To this day I do not feel that I was cocky in my appraisal; bold, yes, but cocky, no. I simply believed that with my level of experience, the proper training and preparation, hard work, flexibility, a burning desire and fierce determination to succeed I could, no, would, achieve my goal someday. I could literally visualize myself in the role of vice president-REO manager for GWB. Here was another opportunity to put my *Winning-Ways to Peak Performance* to work for me. I was very excited about my prospects. Whenever I made the mistake of telling others my goal, however, they skeptically scoffed at the idea. I began vocalizing my, "Yes I can, yes I will, just watch me," mantra. I believed deeply that all the struggles I had between working for Nathan Shapell and taking on this new consulting assignment, coupled with all that I had learned during my vocational life would now start paying dividends. I gladly embraced the challenge. I knew where I'd been and I didn't want to go back.

One of the first marketing ideas I developed for the REO department was a branding initiative for GWB REOs. In the early and mid-'90s most lenders and loan servicers acted as though they didn't have an REO inventory. GWB was no different. Most of these institutions would not allow their real estate listing agents to put, "Bank Owned" or "Foreclosure" on their yard signage, nor in their ads or in the multiple listing service (MLS). They believed, and rightfully so, that buyers would expect deep discounts on properties foreclosed on by the banks, especially if those properties were in fair or poor condition. They didn't want to broadcast to the world that they had a growing non-performing real estate asset problem. Contrarian that I am, however, I believed that because we rehabbed nearly all of our REO properties before we put them on the market through our real estate agent network, our homes would be in much better condition than the properties owned by other institutions. This made our homes more attractive to buyers and increased the potential for selling them at higher prices faster than the competition. Time is money in the REO business. So I proposed introducing the "Great Western Owned" branding program for all rehabbed REOs in our inventory. We would not hide from the fact that we had REOs; we would advertise it to the home-buying public. John Haltom and his superiors bought off on my plan.

Another innovative program we launched entailed a focused strategy for higher-end properties, which back in the mid-1990s started at about $500,000 and went up to $2 million-plus. The idea was to take a close look at each property, especially any that had been on the market but generated little or no interest. I would determine if there was more that needed to be done to rehab or even slightly remodel the house to make it more marketable. Upon deciding what additional work would be required, such as remodeling a kitchen or master bedroom, or tearing up carpet to reveal hardwood floors that we could refinish, add crown molding, etc., etc., we would take the property off the market and complete the work. Following the completion of the work we put the house back on the market at a significantly higher price than we felt the property was worth for two weeks. We then had our listing agent promote the fact that they would soon be holding a special broker open house, with food (if you feed them, they will come), and publicize that a bank executive would be at the open house to make a special announcement about a new marketing strategy.

On the appointed day of the open house we always had terrific food available and the house and grounds were neat and shining clean. When it came time for my announcement I would tell the attending brokers and agents, which was always a large number of Realtors, that we were reducing the listing price by a significant amount (but still above market value). Then I told them that if they sold the house in 30 days or less and then closed escrow within 30 days the selling-side commission would be six percent. That meant there was the potential for the listing agent to make nine percent if they double-ended the deal. That means they represented both the seller and the buyer in the transaction. But even if the listing agent didn't double-end the deal the selling agent who represented the buyer would get twice the commission that is typically paid by sellers. The attending brokers and agents practically scrambled for the door to get back to their offices to call any potential buyers they had been working with in this price range.

This was a very successful program that we initiated on high-end properties all over the United States. We shortened the days on market of these properties and increased the net recovery of money back to GWB through this program. We often made the new loans on the properties as well, adding to our portfolio of performing loans. To my knowledge, no other lender or servicer has ever initiated a similar program. I don't have a clue as to why not, because it was so successful.

(L to R) Scott, me, Kathy, Chris and Diana on Scott and Kristin's wedding day (Photograph by Carolyn Abacherli).

1993 was also eventful for another, more important reason; our oldest son, Scott married his high school sweetheart, Kristin McIntyre on September 18th. Kristin is an unmistakably beautiful and intelligent young woman who resembled Kathy at that same age (and still does). We don't try to analyze this, of course, we are just proud to have this wonderful person in our lives. She has been a model wife to Scott and an exceptional mother to their two children, our grandchildren, Payton, who was born on September 27, 1995 and Tanner, who was born on May 7, 1998. Both of these special children are exceedingly smart, beautiful and loving children who today live on the east coast with their parents. We don't get to see them as often as we would like, which is something we are working on changing as I write this.

Payton has grown to be a striking young lady who participates in her high school marching band on the flag-girl squad. She is a very good student who has worked hard to keep her studies up while participating in other extracurricular activities.

Tanner is our "dancing machine," and an exceptional student in his own right. He is a master at many different video games and he has also played youth soccer and baseball for many years. Both are cherished gifts from God.

Scott, Kristin and the kids are an extremely close-knit, loving family and we are proud of each of them in so many ways.

―――

John Haltom had also put me in charge of our auction program at Great Western Bank. Because our inventory was growing so quickly we needed to dispose of more properties each month and the auction process was a good vehicle to accomplish this. The sales prices tended to be somewhat lower through auctions on average, but the holding time was dramatically reduced. The non-performing asset ratio (the number of non-performing mortgage loans as a percentage of the overall number of loans on a bank's balance sheet) is generally considered acceptable if that ratio is below 1.5 percent, and preferably below 1 percent. The non-performing asset ratio at GWB in 1994 climbed to just over five percent, clearly unacceptable. Auctions were one disposition methodology that could take some pressure off and help reduce that ratio.

One of the major contributing factors to this unacceptable ratio was the aftermath of the Northridge earthquake, which occurred on January 17, 1994. A devastating 6.7 magnitude earthquake that had its epicenter practically right underneath the GWB headquarters, this natural disaster caused more than 33 deaths and over $20 billion in damages throughout the San Fernando Valley and surrounding communities. This resulted in increased foreclosure activity because so many people didn't have earthquake insurance and couldn't afford to repair their homes, thus many of them walked away from their loans. Through a long, focused effort to help modify loans or at the very least offer forbearance to borrowers, GWB and other major lenders mitigated losses to both homeowners and themselves. I also served on the Earthquake Loss Mitigation Committee to provide input on property valuations and other considerations.

The aforementioned marketing programs I introduced proved very effective and I was learning more and more about the mortgage loan default servicing process. I was excited to be contributing to the REO department's success. I was now so deeply involved with GWB that I found I had little time to devote to my ERA clients. Following the Northridge earthquake I decided to discontinue my relationships with them, somewhat regrettably, but for the greater good, or so I hoped. After all, I was on another mission.

To accelerate the disposition of our REO properties GWB had entered into an agreement with a Wall Street investment group for the purpose of selling them portions of our REO inventory in bulk. They had already purchased non-performing loans in large numbers but all parties felt that selling REOs in bulk was another option. The Wall Street firm began buying $40 million worth of REOs from us at a time, which eventually turned out to be a monthly transaction. When you sell 250 properties per month to one buyer and close the sale in 30 days, there is no longer a need to employ as many people as we had in the REO department. We especially didn't need so many people overseeing the rehab process since these bulk-sale properties are sold in their "as-is" condition and therefore were not rehabbed. Layoffs within our ranks began in earnest.

Towards the end of my one-year contract, GWB executive management rolled out a down-sizing initiative for all of loan servicing. I wasn't sure what the term "down-sizing" meant, but it sure sounded like additional layoffs were going to be a big part of this initiative. I didn't realize how right I would prove to be. With our non-performing asset ratio falling, but still above 3.5 percent, and our cost-per-loan far exceeding banking industry standards, GWB was ripe for a takeover by other major institutions. This down-sizing effort would hopefully correct much of our problems and increase stock prices, making us less vulnerable.

Now, I was a consultant. Consultants are generally among the first people released in corporate America during these cost-cutting efforts. I had survived the initial layoffs associated with the bulk sales of REOs, but things weren't looking so promising now. How was I going to get promoted to run the REO department if I wasn't an employee, and worse, if I was released? My plan to learn as much as I could about the REO process, be in the right place at the right time, and be prepared for promotional opportunities were now in jeopardy of being cut short; flexibility was needed now more than ever. I decided to be bold once again, taking the initiative to improve my prospects of achieving my goal.

Several months prior to this program being rolled out, John Haltom had been promoted to default manager and he thus promoted another individual to take over the responsibilities of running the REO department, reporting directly to John. This person was a great guy who had already been in the REO arena for over 15 years, serving as REO manager for several well-known lenders in Southern California. He was a fountain of knowledge. Because of the layoffs resulting from the monthly bulk sale process, the remaining staff had their workloads dramatically increased. It would only increase further because of the down-sizing effort. No more so than for the new REO manager, who I noticed was practically buried under paperwork and had to work late most evenings because of the myriad meetings he had to attend in addition to his increased workload.

I approached the new REO manager with my latest idea; I told him that because he had become so incredibly busy, and because he would be more so following additional layoffs, he needed someone to be his assistant. Someone to take some of the pressure off of him by doing the many things he didn't have time to get to. And special projects that arose constantly; anything that would make the REO manager more efficient and not have to work late so often. I was just trying to plant a seed (once again) so he knew I wanted to help him. I was willing to take on tedious work while continuing to learn as much as I could to increase my value to the company. He said he liked the idea and would think about it. With step one completed I hoped I'd hear back in a week or two as to what his decision would be so I could rest a little easier.

To my surprise, but delight, the REO manager called me into his office the very next day after I had expressed my idea to him. He said he had already discussed it with John, who liked the idea very much. The REO manager said he wanted me to become his, "right-hand man." I immediately saw the humor in his remark, as well as recognizing what a tremendous step forward this would be. Here I was a consultant who was being hired as a full-time employee during one of the biggest down-sizing efforts the bank had ever experienced. The journey would continue. Take the initiative. Be bold.

Chapter Fifteen

More Opportunities… Marching On

"Don't be so humble. You're not that great."
— Golda Meier

More Opportunities...Marching On

I OFFICIALLY BEGAN MY CAREER as an employee of Great Western Bank in their REO department in the summer of 1994. I was now the special assistant to the REO manager. Although my official title was "asset manager" I did not actually manage a portfolio of REO properties at this point. My job was to do whatever tasks I was assigned by my boss and to take pressure off of him by doing so. It was the best possible position to be in to ensure that I learned as much as possible about the REO process; from acquisition of the properties through foreclosure, to the management, marketing, sales and closings on the non-performing residential real estate assets. For the next several months I performed numerous tasks that were menial at best, but the opportunity to learn from the REO manager was extraordinary and I made the most of it during the months ahead.

In mid-February of 1995 I discovered that there was another loan servicing initiative about to be rolled out. Price Waterhouse, a successful London-based professional services and accounting firm had been brought in by executive management at GWB to direct a program widely known as "re-engineering." This project was designed to help further bring down operational expenses, streamline processes and, of course restructure our loan servicing operations. John Haltom had been selected to manage the re-engineering program in cooperation with the team of professionals who worked for Price Waterhouse. They would direct the entire effort. I didn't understand the project's full scope, but I had heard enough to know that no matter what they called it, the net effect was going to be another round of major layoffs. I also heard that there was going to be a team selected from among the different departments that made up loan servicing; collections, loss mitigation, foreclosure and REO. They would work hand-in-hand with the Price Waterhouse team. I instantly decided that it had to better to be a "re-engineer" rather than be "re-engineered"... out. I volunteered to interview for a spot on the team.

The two young men who would serve as the team liaisons between the GWB team and the Price Waterhouse team did the interviewing. They made the mistake of asking me to tell them "a little bit" about myself. I told them everything they wanted to know about me and more, including my background in business, my experience playing Little League Baseball, football and everything else I could think of to impress upon them that I was someone who could benefit this process and ultimately GWB. John soon told me they were duly impressed. I had been selected by Price Waterhouse and approved by GWB management to participate on the re-engineering team.

There's no need to belabor all that transpired during this lengthy, involved process. It is enough to say that we went through intensive training to familiarize ourselves with all aspects of a re-engineering program; to learn about the various procedures involved, including process mapping and the creation of findings replete with documented projected savings in terms of overhead expenses and gains in efficiencies. We then spent many weeks and months researching current policies, procedures and processes, as well as current organizational structures. We interviewed countless "stakeholders," developed recommendations for improving interconnected processes to eliminate unnecessary handoffs and established improved, more efficient organizational structures. As a team, we worked very closely with one another on a daily basis since we were relieved of our normal day-to-day responsibilities. This was difficult to do in my case because the REO manager had grown so accustomed to my daily assistance.

The Price Waterhouse team had extensive knowledge of all aspects of loan servicing... except the REO process. This was a blessing for me. I had free rein to re-engineer the REO department the way I believed it should be after interviewing people in our company as well as seeking out best practices from other institutions. In order to better ensure that I would have "buy-in" from the remaining members of the REO department, and especially my manager, I recruited our top asset managers to be part of an REO-based re-engineering team. That way the recommendations that would emerge would be seen as a collective effort and not the ideas of one person. That proved to be one of the single most important decisions I made in this process.

When it was all said and done we successfully re-engineered the REO department; its organizational structure, policies and procedures, and business processes. We had done so in a manner that ultimately saved GWB several millions of dollars the following year. The other departments devolved back practically as they had been prior to re-engineering once Price Waterhouse had left the scene. The REO department re-engineering was completed and implemented before the other departments, so I was the first member of the re-engineering team to return to my duties on a regular basis. It is worth noting that of all the default servicing departments that restructured themselves and supposedly streamlined their processes, only the changes made to the REO department stuck beyond a year's time.

One of the most important outcomes of re-engineering the REO department was the organizational structure. I eliminated layers of management, more fully empowering the asset managers to perform their duties. We split the nationwide inventory up into five regions, each headed by a senior asset manager. Because of the successful outcome of the REO department re-engineering, I was promoted to senior asset manager for the South Central/East L.A. Region, one of the largest and most challenging regions in the country.

I had enhanced my visibility to senior and executive management throughout this process by successfully re-engineering our department. I gradually took on more of the decision-making responsibilities within the REO department. Over time I became a bit more aggressive in this regard after the REO manager told me he was reluctant to down-size any further, despite clear signs that we again needed to do so since our inventory continued to decrease in size. He told me he wanted to retire from GWB, and didn't want to make waves. My charge was to do what I felt was in the best interests of the institution; be bold and not hold back on helping my boss to make the tough decisions. I tried to persuade him to be more proactive, but he just wouldn't do so. I felt it was my duty to let management know that I recognized what needed to be done. I didn't want them to think that I was also reluctant to make tough choices or do what needed to be done.

More Opportunities...Marching On

About six months after the re-engineering program concluded, a new senior manager was hired by executive management to oversee all of loan servicing. A new default manager was also hired. The senior manager immediately took stock of the management team he inherited and determined that some of the managers were not performing up to his high standards. As a result, my direct supervisor, the REO manager, had been asked to find a new career opportunity... with another company. I was subsequently named REO manager in his place.

My goal to become the next REO manager was realized in just over two years of employment at GWB. To those who had felt that I was crazy to believe that I would one day become the REO manager for Great Western Bank I could only smile at them in their absence. I was among the very few of us who had not only survived down-sizing, right-sizing and re-engineering, but had thrived and accomplished another major goal. And I accomplished it by sticking to the same principles that worked before; playing semi-pro football to get a tryout with an NFL team; becoming director of market research and then director of advertising and public relations for Shapell Industries, Inc., and in a rather less successful way becoming a marketing consultant to builders, developers, real estate companies and mortgage lenders throughout Southern California. But more challenges were just around the corner; more success, but also another failure... at least it appeared to be at the time.

For the next several months I served as Vice President – REO manager for Great Western Bank. That all too soon became a tenuous existence. Home Savings of America announced its intentions on the front page of the *Los Angeles Times* to virtually absorb Great Western Bank through a hostile takeover. Charlie Rheinhart, Home Savings of America's chief executive officer was quoted in the piece as saying that Home Savings' superior business model, management team and performance level on behalf of their shareholders made this move possible. He also stated that the takeover would surely result in massive layoffs to fully benefit from the consolidation of these two mortgage lending giants. He made it clear that the employees of Home Savings had little to fear regarding these pending layoffs. GWB employees on the other hand should basically start looking for work elsewhere.

Our executive management team did not appreciate Rheinhart's statements blasted out through the *L.A. Times*. Having a desire to cut a better deal for GWB's shareholders, they boarded the company jet and flew up to meet with Washington Mutual CEO, Kerry Killinger to try to strike that better deal. They succeeded. Almost overnight the Home Savings takeover dissolved and GWB became part of the growing number of banks that were now flying the banner of Washington Mutual Bank (WaMu).

My next challenge would be to remain REO manager. Just prior to buying GWB, WaMu had purchased American Savings Bank, which was also headquartered in Southern California. American Savings had all the same departments that GWB had, with personnel and managers in each that mirrored ours, at least in terms of departmental structure. But we both did business a bit differently, particularly with respect to REO management and disposition. Our REO portfolios were roughly the same size, but GWB's was a bit larger. However, I had less than half the number of people working in my REO department than American Savings. The main reason for that was my mastering the use of third-party asset management outsource companies to assist in the management and disposition of our properties. I didn't outsource the entire inventory because I wanted my two outsource companies to not only compete with each other, but also to compete against the direct brokers (real estate agents and brokers who were assigned REO properties directly from the bank). GWB was the ultimate beneficiary of this balanced disposition strategy because of this competition. I was one of the pioneers in our industry to utilize asset management outsourcing in a big way.

It made much more sense to me to endeavor as best I could to keep my internal operating expenses as fixed as possible. With REO inventories constantly fluctuating up and down, especially in an environment where you could instantly grow your portfolio through acquisition, I felt it made more sense to hire outsource companies to help us manage the REO process. Let them add staff or lay people off as necessary. This was the successful strategy we employed at GWB. To me, going direct to the real estate brokers exclusively to manage and dispose of all REOs was inefficient and more costly.

For many months the two groups worked independently until such time as WaMu management would determine who would stay and who would go. It was a frustrating, stressful existence, but we made the most of it. All the while fighting hard to convince WaMu's senior managers that my balanced disposition strategy was superior to not only American Savings REO disposition methodology, but also to WaMu's in their Seattle headquarters (each operation had separate REO departments at that point).

In the end, I was named REO manager of the consolidated companies. We brought over a few of the American Savings REO personnel, but the vast majority was released. Senior management at WaMu initially instructed me to have no more than ten percent of our inventory outsourced. Over time I proved through our key performance indicators (the bottom line) that our balanced disposition strategy was superior to their own. They ultimately left me alone to manage the combined portfolio as I believed it should be. I never had less than 50 percent of the inventory outsourced. This came in quite handy upon our next bank consolidation (This next part is really fun for me to write about).

Less than two years after Charlie Rheinhart's announcement of his intentions to facilitate a hostile takeover of GWB, Home Savings of America itself was struggling. They were subsequently purchased by... *WaMu!* The new announcement was music to our ears. There would be no doubt about who would survive this latest consolidation of operations; we were in the driver's seat and I was immediately named REO manager over the combined inventories.

Almost immediately our portfolio would double in size. I hired a few of the Home Savings REO personnel to join us in Chatsworth. Most were given a termination package. It wasn't pleasant to let them go. Changing people's lives in such a way never is, but it certainly occurred to me how ironic it was that so many Home Savings employees were now out of work.

Sorry Charlie.

Over the next twelve months my dedicated team, especially Sue McNalley, who became my "work wife" so to speak, because of how close we became as a team, continued to perform at high levels. We became a well-oiled machine and produced results that were beyond the expectations of management and they therefore did not interfere in any way with our operation. This was further validation that my disposition strategy was sound, as was my management style. Things hummed along quite nicely.

By the middle of 1999 our inventory was shrinking rather rapidly. The success we enjoyed in the REO department at Great Western Bank and subsequently Washington Mutual was the result of superior teamwork and dedication to excellence by my staff. My leadership was a factor, to be sure, but it was the people around me who deserve the lion's share of credit. Having been a part of four championship football teams I knew intimately the power of teamwork. I stressed it all the time as a manager. Individual performance is important, but it cannot replace the synergy of a committed, dedicated team all working toward the same goals and objectives.

Never wanting upper management to come to me and ask why my staff was too large for the work at hand, I proactively released another round of asset managers and support staff. This was getting to be more distasteful over time, but it was part of my responsibilities. I did so because it was what I felt best served my employer.

My workload was fast diminishing. I was beginning to feel it was time for a new challenge. Again, I don't know the reason behind my inability to be satisfied with success once I had achieved it. It is what it is. I also continued to seek out motivational speaking opportunities because I felt compelled to do so. My experiences while employed by GWB and WaMu added value to my motivational presentation because I could relate that my individual achievements in business were a direct result of learning from my achievements in sports. I had achieved my major goals several times now, proving that luck alone could not be the sole cause; quite the contrary.

I had been contacted by a couple of executive search firms in mid-1999 and interviewed with other banks that were looking for an REO manager. One of the banks that I interviewed with was located in Pennsylvania. I was interviewed by several senior managers and it seemed to go quite well. Kathy and I had never lived outside California, but our kids were all grown by this time and we contemplated moving across the country if an appropriate career opportunity presented itself. This one nearly did. The company was prepared to make me an offer, but they were in the middle of a potential merger, so the final decision would have to await the disposition of that potentiality. It looked imminent that I would be changing jobs and we would be relocating.

However, in late 1998 I had approached the people at the Southern California Chapter of the March of Dimes to see about getting involved in their fundraising activities. I had long had an affinity for their mission to help fight birth defects and had done some fundraising for them. I now had more free time resulting from the consolidations being behind us and the declining foreclosure activity. Our inventory was also declining as mentioned above. I wanted to help the March of Dimes. Since I was planning on doing much more public speaking in the future, I also felt that any publicity I could generate in the process of raising money wouldn't hurt.

Over lunch with two representatives from the March of Dimes in October of '98 the two ladies thanked me for my interest in helping them raise funds not only to help fight birth defects but also to prevent premature births. They then told me that their biggest fundraising activity each year was their nationwide *WalkAmerica* event. I asked who had raised the most money in Southern California as an individual in 1998. They said that a young lady from Los Angeles raised over $10,000 for *WalkAmerica*. I told them that I would make every effort to top that number in 1999, because I had just had a sudden flash of inspiration: I had been asked by some escrow companies, Realtor associations and other real estate-related companies to give my motivational presentation to their employees at awards dinners, Christmas parties and so forth. They were prepared to pay me to do so. I had declined their requests because of potential conflict-of-interest issues related to my position at WaMu. I asked these two nice ladies if I could apply any future speaking fees over the next few months to my 1999 *WalkAmerica* pledges. I said that if these companies still wanted to pay me for speaking I would agree to do so if they made the checks out directly to the March of Dimes. There would be no conflict of interest by doing so. They were skeptical that I could actually achieve the goal of surpassing the $10,000 mark, but liked the idea and said, "Yes."

I had acted, or at least, talked, boldly. I had set another major goal and had the beginnings of a plan to achieve it. I can assure you I was building a deep burning desire to top the $10,000 mark set in 1998. Not only because I wanted to help the March of Dimes, but also because I believed I really could achieve this goal and the publicity around such a worthy accomplishment might help me to expand my speaking opportunities, which was and is my true passion. I was willing to put forth whatever effort was necessary and was determined to succeed.

Over the next several months in addition to being invited to speak at various real estate-related company events, and receive checks made out to the March of Dimes, I coordinated a half-day event I titled the, "Golden Goal Success Seminar." Several title companies and real estate brokers and attorneys sponsored the event. We held it at the Long Beach Marriott Hotel by the Long Beach Airport. We invited brokers and vendors from our REO network and made sure they knew that net proceeds were going to the March of Dimes. I hired several other speakers at reasonable fees to give presentations in addition to the one I would give. We also had a small live auction. We netted about $7,000 for the March of Dimes after all was said and done. It was a pretty decent success.

By the time the 1999 *WalkAmerica* event approached in April, I had amassed over $17,000 for my pledges, but I wasn't done yet. I knew that Washington Mutual had a matching funds program to support their employees' charitable activities, so I called up to our headquarters in Seattle to find out the details. When I asked the manager responsible for this program what the ceiling was that they would match, she said, "We usually match donations of fifty dollars or one-hundred dollars, and sometimes a thousand or more." I said that was great, but asked what was the *most* WaMu would match. She laughed and then said, "The actual maximum is $10,000." Feeling like Sonny Corleone in *The Godfather*, I said, "You mean to tell me that if I raise $10,000 for the March of Dimes, you'll match that amount?" She said, "Yes, absolutely." I immediately filled out the paperwork and attached the proof that I had raised $17,000 already. Within a few days I received a check made out to the March of Dimes for $10,000 signed by WaMu's CEO, Kerry Killinger! I had now helped to raise over $27,000 for this great charity, blowing away the 1998 high mark of $10,000. I ended up being the number one individual fundraiser for *WalkAmerica* in Southern California in 1999 and number three in the nation! But wait, there's even more!

Because of the support that I had received in achieving my goal to be the number one individual fundraiser for the March of Dimes in Southern California, we believed that additional support was possible with respect to fundraising because of the position I held at WaMu. The people at the March of Dimes and I came up with another idea; create a new fundraising event that would honor the "Real Estate Industry Man of the Year." It is true that I had now been involved in the real estate and housing industries for nearly three decades, but it was a stretch to believe that I had accomplished enough to be the recipient of such an honor. The main goal however was to raise money for the March of Dimes. I was simply an individual who might well command the support necessary to make a positive difference.

I helped select a group of hard working, loyal individuals to serve on the event committee (another team effort). I could not personally participate in soliciting contributions, sponsorships or the purchase of tickets to the event. It was hoped by the March of Dimes that enough sponsorships and tickets would be sold to gross $70,000 from this first-of-its-kind fundraising event. I felt we could do better and was committed to seeing to it that we did. At this point I notified the bank in Philadelphia that I was no longer interested in pursuing the position they were offering me, because I needed to be involved in the March of Dimes event.

The committee co-chairs for the Real Estate Industry Man of the Year fundraiser, did a marvelous job heading up our committee. They were also able to get Judge Wopner of *The People's Court* television fame to serve as master of ceremonies for the event. The Judge's participation at the event was a real plus, as was the contribution of long-time television news personality, eight-time Emmy Award-winning broadcaster, Mario Machado.

The co-chairs then secured the Mayor of Los Angeles at the time, Richard Riordan to be our "honorary" chairperson. There were other notable individuals who lent their names to help promote the event as honorary committee members, including John Wooden, George Allen, Junior, USC head football coach, John Robinson, and many, many other well-known Los Angelinos.

The March of Dimes Real Estate Industry Man of the Year Awards Dinner was held on October 21, 1999 at the Hollywood Hilton Hotel adjacent to Universal Studios. It was a formal gala offering delicious food, lively entertainment, a silent auction and, of course, speeches. The committee did such a terrific job promoting the fundraiser that over 600 people were in attendance that evening, including Nathan Shapell who purchased a table for some of his employees with whom I had worked twenty years prior. A tremendous amount of publicity had helped us promote the event, as planned. I also had invited Coaches Crutchfield and Rowland and their wives, as well as Victor Miller to be my special guests. My other guests included my parents, brother Kirk and his wife, Kaye, our sister Valerie, my children and granddaughter, Holly. My son, Chris, had actually helped with the audio-visual requirements of the event and we celebrated his 20th birthday that night with a cake that was rolled out on a special cart during the event where the attendees all joined in singing "Happy Birthday;" It was a special, added touch to the evening.

Following several speeches by those associated with the March of Dimes I was awarded a beautiful plaque and given the opportunity to deliver an acceptance speech.

As I stood before this large crowd of family, friends, high school football coaches, past and present co-workers, my staff from WaMu, and the many real estate agents, brokers, attorneys, vendors and others who were there to support me and the March of Dimes, I knew I did not truly deserve to receive such an honor or be giving a speech. But I also felt this was a once-in-a-lifetime experience and I soaked it all in when the audience applauded. I knew we had done a good thing for a very worthy cause.

With TV cameras rolling from KABC Channel 7 News I gave my speech. I chose to thank my parents, coaches, Nathan Shapell, my staff, the management at WaMu, my children and especially Kathy, for their support throughout my lifetime to that point. I wanted to publicly acknowledge that I could not have achieved any of my major goals without their help and encouragement. I went on and on far longer than one should in such circumstances. A classier thing to do, I now realize, would have been to thank the March of Dimes for the remarkable work that they do, quickly thank the committee for their hard work, and the attendees for their support, and then simply go back to my table and sit down. Hindsight is a wonderful thing.

Learning to endure people's slings and arrows, teasing and bullying in my youth made me more resolute to never allow others to define who I was or what I could accomplish. This special event was no different. The silent auction garnered over $15,000, the highest sum up until that point the March of Dimes had ever collected on a silent auction. In total, through the magnificent hard work of everyone on the event committee and the staff at the March of Dimes, over $140,000 was raised for this worthwhile charitable organization, netting them over $100,000. Whether I was worthy or not of receiving such recognition, I nevertheless had achieved another major goal through a team effort. Mission accomplished... once more.

Chapter Sixteen

—

Tenacity Matters

"Most people give up just when they're about to achieve success, they give up at the last minute of the game, one foot from a winning touchdown."

— H. Ross Perot

I HAVE APPLIED THE PRINCIPLES of the *Winning Ways to Peak Performance* to my most notable vocational pursuits and have achieved my share of success in the business world because of it. My motivational presentation today takes on greater significance to people beyond just being an interesting story about athletic achievements. I explain to audiences across the country that if a somewhat ordinary, flawed person like Lynn Effinger can overcome adversity to ultimately achieve success over and over again, they too can realize their goals in life. And they can do so despite the many challenges they will face. I also emphasize that even when you fail, which we all do at times, you must never give up and never give in. Tenacity matters. That important message would resonate in my own head very soon; and thankfully so.

Following the successful March of Dimes fundraiser I decided to resign from Washington Mutual by year's end. I wanted to pursue a "career" as a full-time motivational speaker, like Zig Ziglar, Anthony Robbins, Les Brown and so many others. I actually thought I could make a living doing so, despite not being a celebrity of any kind. A huge mistake at that point that Kathy had tried her best to help me avoid making, but I had made up my mind. Did I say huge mistake?

After leaving Washington Mutual in early January of 2000 to pursue paid speaking opportunities, I realized real fast that I had been asked to speak at so many venues the past two years because of my position at WaMu; not necessarily because people truly wanted to hear me give my presentation. How naïve could I have been? Because so many people wanted to either secure their position as a vendor for WaMu's REO department, or become one, they had blown enough smoke up my pant leg that I had unfortunately bought into their fawning and accolades. This was very foolish on my part. I had come to believe theirs and my own hype. I must have forgotten the old adage, "Never believe your own press." My swelled head clouded my perspective. Seeing the error in my ways, I also discovered after I left Washington Mutual that I had become, "Lynn who?" All those people who purported to be my "friend" now turned their attentions elsewhere. Needing to secure speaking engagements to have an income, rather than doing so because I loved giving my presentation to motivate and inspire others, and raising money for charity, became far less attractive to me. If I wasn't speaking for the "right reasons" it was not satisfying in the least.

That lack of satisfaction from trying to make a living as a motivational speaker, and the acknowledgement that I had made such a huge personal mistake that would again negatively impact my wife and son, Chris who was living with us while working and going to college hit me hard. I went into the deepest depressive state of my life. Maybe not in the clinical sense, but I was in a major funk nonetheless. In the midst of another nationwide recession I found myself unemployed with no prospects on the horizon to find employment. I was back in the lowest valley all too soon after being on the highest peak.

It took many months of searching for a new position within the REO arena. In the meantime I had earned my California Real Estate Salesperson's license and worked at several new home communities as a "host." Not a well-paying gig and quite boring, but at least I was gainfully employed. In early September of 2001, representatives from Traveler's Bank & Trust in Hanover, Maryland, which was part of Citigroup, responded to a resume I had sent to them regarding a position as asset manager in their REO department. They reviewed my work history and credentials and asked me to interview for REO *manager* instead; a new opening that had just been created. Following a successful interview over the telephone, they asked me to fly to Maryland to have a face-to-face interview. Everything was arranged for me to fly to Maryland... on September 13, 2001. Needless to say, the tragic, horrifying events of 9/11 put that interview, and most everything else, on hold.

Just a couple of weeks or so after 9/11 I made the trip to Maryland and was subsequently hired to manage the REO department for Travelers. The foreclosure and REO departments at Travelers Bank & Trust had both been managed by one person up until I had been hired as REO manager. This had worked just fine for quite some time until the foreclosure rate began to escalate. Their inventory of bank-owned properties began to swell. In late 2001 the bank projected that the REO inventory was growing at a pace that would cause it to more than double in less than 12 months. This rate of growth meant that it was time to split out the two departments so that a new manager could focus on the disposition of REO properties. The previous manager who was overseeing both departments had far more experience with the foreclosure process than the REO process. It made total sense for him to focus on that aspect of default servicing while they hired an expert to focus on REO. Ergo, my opportunity arose to join this division of Citigroup, which at that time was one of the most profitable corporations in the world.

When I arrived in Maryland to take on this new challenge the existing staff was somewhat small. There were mostly inexperienced people in place trying to manage the listing, marketing, property management, sales and closings on bank-owned real estate. These were subprime loans on non-performing real estate assets that were mostly in fair to poor condition, or worse. The average sales price was under $60,000. These properties are tough to sell and require experienced professionals to manage the process to minimize holding time and maximize the net return against the loan balance. As it was, because of the location and condition of most of these properties, the bank was losing an average of approximately 35 percent of the amount owed on each property. It could be higher if untrained people were managing the process. My first challenge was to retrain the staff. If anyone was not willing or able to perform up to the high standards that I was accustomed to, they would be worked with until they improved or would be weeded out in the best interests of the team and the bank. The inventory turn rate, which is the number of properties sold and closed each month as a percentage of the overall current inventory at the start of each month had been around 15 percent before I was hired. The industry standard at the time was 20 percent. I had to get us there, and fast if we were to get a handle on the rapidly growing inventory.

The success we enjoyed at Washington Mutual was due in large part to having an experienced, tight-knit team of professionals managing each phase of the REO disposition process. And also because we employed my balanced disposition strategy to help us manage the entire process while keeping our operational expenses as close to fixed as possible. Since our inventory at Traveler's was growing so quickly we had to either add staff or increase the percentage of properties that were outsourced. They had one outsource company in place when I was hired, but I quickly determined that they were not performing up to my high standards. I did add a few people internally. I also replaced a few existing staff members who would not or could not meet our performance standards. But I knew we needed another outsource partner to help us perform at the highest possible level without adding significantly to our operating expenses.

I called the owner of one of the outsource companies I had hired while at GWB and WaMu that had performed well for us. I asked him if he'd be willing to work for Travelers. They were only managing a handful of properties at the time, so they were quite eager to serve. I was not going to tell my superiors that I was bringing in another outsource company. As with most of my career, I decided that I would rather ask for forgiveness if a decision I made did not turn out positively rather than permission to make a decision that I was convinced was in the best interest of my employer. I needed a company I could trust would manage the process exactly as I wanted it to. This turned out to be one of my best decisions while in the employ of Citi/Travelers.

Within months we had retrained our staff, built an incredibly tight-knit team, got our arms around the growing inventory and increased our inventory turn rate from 15 percent to more than 20 percent. Despite the increased turn rate we also decreased the losses against the loan balances by more than five percent. Our new outsource partner played a valuable role in not only helping us manage the inventory, but their superior performance on our behalf made the other outsource company improve their performance. The ultimate beneficiary of this, of course, was the bank.

I would not have been able to achieve success at Travelers Bank & Trust, which later became Citicorp Trust Bank, without the loyal, dedicated staff that worked in our department. This was particularly true of Brad Wachsmuth and especially of Amy Bitz, the two supervisors who reported directly to me. Amy became my go-to person and although we struggled a bit early on to develop a solid working relationship, in time we became not only an awesome management team, she became a life-long friend whom I admire tremendously. The team we grew and trained became one of the most effective and efficient in the entire organization and one of the best in the entire default servicing industry. It was very gratifying to replicate the success I had enjoyed at GWB/WaMu and prove once again that my success and the success of my team were not a fluke or the result of luck.

In late 2003 Citi decided to begin consolidating its REO operation in Hanover with their larger operation in Coppell, Texas. Kathy and I did not want to relocate to that great state at that time, so I left Citi to take on another career opportunity. We wanted to eventually return to California so Kathy and I could be closer to our children and grandchildren once again.

On September 20, 2003 our youngest son, Chris, married Amber Ruiz, a very welcome addition to our family. And on October 11, 2004 we were all joined by Ian Christopher Effinger (I call him the Iceman because of his initials). Ian is a remarkable little boy who thinks I am quite special indeed (the feeling is mutual). So much so, in fact, that on opening day of the Major League Baseball season in 2010 as we headed in Chris's van to see the Arizona Diamondbacks play the San Diego Padres Ian said something that rocked my world. After talking on and on about this, that and the other thing, out of the blue Ian said to me, "Hey Papa, guess what?" I answered, "What Ian." He replied, "When I grow up I want to have a hand just like yours." I gave him a big hug and smiled, then said, "I love you, Ian." He and I are as close as a grandson and Papa could possibly be and I thank the Lord for sending him to us all.

Chris is not only a wonderful son, he is a good friend. We have had many exciting road trips and other adventures together over the years, especially when we lived in Maryland. He is one of the most interesting, smart and humorous individuals with whom I have ever spent time. It is tremendously satisfying to witness his transformation into fatherhood. One of the hardest working members of his generation that I know, he has been building a solid career in the mortgage banking industry himself. Today he works as an underwriter for one of the nation's largest and most successful mortgage lenders. His wife, Amber, is a wonderful young lady who is a loving, caring wife and mother who is universally liked by those with whom she works in property management, as well as her customers. We are delighted and proud to have her in our nuclear family.

(L to R) Kristin, Tanner, Scott and Payton on Christmas Eve of 2001.

Tenacity Matters

Amber and Chris just before they were married in 2003.

(L to R) My grandson, Ian (The Iceman), me and Chris.

Our wonderful grandchildren (Clockwise from the back – Holly, Tanner, Ian and Payton in Kathy's favorite Christmas gift in 2006).

Holly's high school graduation picture in May of 2011.

Me and Kathy at my 30th High School Reunion in 1998.

Before finally heading back to California, I accepted the position of Director of REO Services for Safeguard Properties, the leading provider of property preservation services in America. They were located in Brooklyn Heights, Ohio. This was not my finest hour, as the company and I turned out to be a poor fit. I did my best to prosper there for as long as I could, and did have a degree of success, but ultimately decided to move on. Another influencing factor was that Kathy had become quite ill and needed surgery. We concluded that it would be best to have that important surgery in California to be near our family in case things did not work out as hoped.

I subsequently took a position as operations manager for a real estate valuation services provider in San

Diego County that was a subsidiary of First American Corporation. This enabled us to move back to our home state. Fortunately, Kathy's surgery was a success, although she lost 75 percent use of one of her kidneys. I had been scared to death that I might lose her. I would be absolutely lost without her.

I had taken both these positions in another reactive rather than proactive manner, which rarely works out in a positive way. After helping to build this company's default services valuation division and bringing in clients I had known throughout my tenure in the industry, the company signed a huge contract with a major national lender. The CEO transferred the staff I had helped train to cover the needs of this new client. This had an adverse impact on the clients I had secured for this company and I decided that my reputation was at stake. I decided to extricate myself after having been there for 18 months and began my job search anew.

After several weeks of interviews I decided that perhaps it was time to retire from the REO business. This also became apparent because after looking for another management opportunity in REO I was not able to get hired in California. The only open positions for which I was not considered to be overqualified (although I was willing to take them) were outside of our state. So soon after returning home, Kathy did not want to relocate to another area at that point. I then decided to go in a much different direction.

Back in 1978 while I worked for Nathan Shapell I had been offered an opportunity to go to work for the Los Angeles Chapter of the March of Dimes. I was honored to be considered to join this important non-profit organization and was excited about the possibility of building a career within this wonderful, highly respected institution. I was making significantly more money at Shapell than the March of Dimes could pay me, which was the only drawback. After careful consideration and lengthy discussions with Kathy I declined their offer because I had a growing young family and felt that although I would have loved to work for them I just couldn't do it at that time. In 2006, however, our children were grown and they were building lives of their own. With our family financial situation in far better shape than it had ever been, I felt I could now afford to take a lower salary if it meant serving the community through employment with a non-profit organization. I looked at it as if I were "semi-retired" and didn't have to work; I *wanted* to work, but in this type of capacity.

I anticipated finding a position with fewer fiscal responsibilities, no managerial pressures and much less stress than I had become accustomed to in default servicing. It would be a nice break from what I had been doing. As a result, I became an area representative for the Blood Bank of San Bernardino and Riverside Counties in September of 2006. As an area rep it was my responsibility to go out into the community and meet with business owners, managers, corporations, schools and places of worship to secure locations and support for mobile blood drives. While it was a serious adjustment to go from managing multi-million dollar portfolios of real estate assets and a large staff of people, I eventually settled in to my new career in the non-profit world. It was one of the most rewarding experiences of my adult life. My presentation skills and networking experience paid off handsomely in this new position. My expectation was that I would work for the Blood Bank until I could work no more; never considering actual retirement. I also believed that I could step up my search for motivational speaking opportunities in this kind of position, which turned out to be true.

Early on in this position I decided that a great way to increase the number of opportunities to book mobile blood drives would be to become very involved in the local chambers of commerce. This strategy proved very effective in less than a year on the job. I was the only one of seven area reps to employ it. I became so active in these chambers and met so many wonderful people who shared my interest in serving our community that I increased the number of mobile blood drives in my territory by over 45 percent that first year. The support I received from the presidents and staffs of the chambers helped me fast-track my efforts on behalf of the Blood Bank. I served as an Ambassador and as Publisher of the Murrieta Chamber of Commerce's newsletter and served on other committees as well. For the Temecula Valley Chamber of Commerce I was an Ambassador and served on several committees, including as Vice-Chairman and Chairman of a couple. As a result of my efforts, and the professionalism of our mobile teams, the Blood Bank was named "Non-Profit Organization of the Year" by the Temecula Valley Chamber of Commerce. I received the "Chairman's Choice Award" from the Murrieta Chamber of Commerce. The Blood Bank, which later changed its name to LifeStream, was also nominated as "Business of the Year" by the Murrieta Chamber of Commerce. The increased profile of LifeStream was critical in my area because the San Diego Blood Bank and the Red Cross also served the communities I was involved in.

A side benefit to my association with the Blood Bank was that I decided to become a regular blood donor. You are literally helping to save lives when you donate blood, and I encourage you to do so if you haven't already. Out of the roughly 65 percent of the population who are eligible to donate blood, less than 5 percent actually do. Donating blood is an unselfish way to give of yourself to help others in need, and it doesn't cost you anything.

In February of 2009 amidst one of the worst housing crises and economic downturns in American history, the president and owner of the third-party REO outsource company that I had hired to work for us at Travelers Bank & Trust in 2001 asked me to represent his company on a consulting basis. He wanted me to be in charge of all marketing and new business development activities. He had recently lost one of his biggest clients and had rarely done any marketing, advertising or networking to promote his business. He now *desperately* needed someone to help quickly raise their profile within the industry and hopefully bring in new business. I was quite content at LifeStream and wasn't looking for a change, but I agreed to help him as an independent contractor. We had worked together for Great Western Bank and he eventually reported to me as an asset manager when I was the REO Manager for GWB and Washington Mutual. He and I had known each other since 1993 and became good friends. When a friend needs you, you answer the call.

For several months I functioned in both capacities, as area representative for LifeStream and as a consultant to the asset management company. However, the travel required by my responsibilities at the outsource company meant something had to give as I ran out of personal time off at LifeStream. I reluctantly made the tough decision to leave the blood bank and work full time for the outsource company in October of 2009. Everything happens for a reason.

My return to the REO arena once again and my chances for success would, of course, require the following, as by now you should know very well:

- Be bold - set goals and have a plan,
- Develop a burning desire and a passion to achieve my goal,
- Be willing to work hard and sacrifice,
- Be flexible and embrace change, and
- Be determined to overcome adversity to succeed.

Returning to the industry in which I had thrived for nearly fifteen years, but had been away from for just over two, would prove to be a good move for me. The goals I immediately set were: (a) Get involved in the REO Managers Association (REOMAC), (b) Advertise, (c) Develop press releases for trade association publications, (d) Have a booth at selected trade shows and industry conferences, (e) Write articles for trade publications that would help establish industry knowledge and increase exposure for the outsource company, (f) Make contact with past associates and continually network with them, as well as others in the industry that might be aware of potential clients, (g) Participate on industry panels and as a featured speaker at various seminars, conferences and other default servicing industry meetings to cost-effectively raise our profile in the marketplace, and (h) make cold calls to as many potential clients as possible.

As I got deeply involved in the industry once again, I realized how much I missed it, and the people. I would not have left my job at LifeStream had I not once again developed a burning desire and passion for succeeding as a consultant to this company in need. This, despite knowing that representing an asset management company that only had one existing client (which I had actually brought to them when I was the REO Manager at Citi in 2001) would be quite a difficult task. Adding to the challenge was the fact and that they didn't offer valuation services (broker price opinions), or had rarely ever networked or actively marketed themselves to potential clients. This was to be a tough sell. Especially now that there were so many newer, larger, more marketing-savvy outsource companies in the marketplace. The biggest positives, in addition to my many contacts in the industry, was the quality of service the company had provided to several of the nation's largest mortgage lenders over the years, and the quality of their staff. Having helped them become a best-in-class outsource company when they worked for us at Citi and because of their consistent performance on behalf of Citi for nearly a decade, I was more than comfortable soliciting new clients for them.

I was willing to sacrifice my comfort zone at home in order to travel. I often flew clear across the country to the various trade shows, meetings and industry conferences required by my consulting position. I knew it would be hard work to achieve success because of the aforementioned challenges. But, no pain, no gain.

Because the REO business and default servicing are inherently replete with constant change, I expected to be as flexible as possible to "go with the flow." None of us realized just how much change was in store for this industry and in this country. Most importantly I was determined to overcome adversity as I came upon it to achieve success for the firm, and subsequently for myself as well.

My renewed involvement in a high-profile position within the mortgage loan default servicing industry, combined with my extensive background in this business led to numerous opportunities to serve as a featured speaker and expert panelist at various industry-related seminars and conferences. I was once again one of the most well-known executives in the industry. As a result, opportunities to write articles for industry trade journals also came to me. Eventually, I was asked to serve as Editor for the REO Manager's Association's (REOMAC) newsletter. This was another high-profile opportunity. As stated above, this had been part of my strategy from the outset. It became an even more important area of marketing focus because the owner of the outsource company was reluctant or unable to spend money on advertising or to pay to have a booth set up at industry conferences, or even be a sponsor at such events. Since he was paying me a monthly retainer fee I was not in a position to complain.

The heightened exposure the company received from my participation at these conferences was something that they had never before come close to achieving. Apparently, they failed to see the value of it. But my continued participation enabled me to attend more industry conferences than planned or budgeted for. Many times my registration fee was waived and/or other expenses were paid for by the host organization, such as meals and lodging, since I would be a panelist or speaker. I was therefore able to maximize our "bang-for-the-buck." It also led to other potential mentoring opportunities and a welcome increase in the number of offers I received to give my motivational speaking presentation. This further elevated my desire to pursue even more speaking engagements and, eventually, to finally write this book.

Misguided interference by the Obama Administration in the housing market by establishing foreclosure moratoria, unsuccessful loan modification programs that actually hurt many homeowners, and other poorly designed programs and regulations, caused foreclosure activity to stall during the better part of my association with this firm; despite the dramatic increase in delinquent loans across the country. On the surface this might seem to be good thing. However, unintended consequences from the fallout of their failure exacerbated the situation significantly. This made securing new clients extremely difficult; not only for us, but also for other outsource companies, real estate agents, title companies, attorneys and others who are highly trained and experienced in this specialized housing discipline.

The economic recovery was actually wounded by these programs, not enhanced, further exacerbating the housing crisis. In fact, largely due to government intervention in the housing sector, while enabling borrowers to remain in their homes without making mortgage payments for as much as two years or more before foreclosing, a double-dip recession, or worse, looms over our future. When this happens it will be the first time in our nation's history that we have experienced a double-dip recession. I have been publicly predicting this outcome for over a year and news reports while I am writing this final chapter in May of 2011 indicate we are nearly there. I am known in this industry as a lone voice of common sense among default servicing executives for a reason; I do not sugar-coat my opinions and strongly held beliefs. I truly call them as I see them.

I was hugely successful at increasing our profile within the default servicing industry. My own visibility also grew significantly along the way. Unfortunately, I was not able to bring in the new business that would have enabled me to continue on in this consulting capacity. The company's owner kept extending my tenure because we *both* believed that we were close to obtaining new clients. It just didn't work out that way. I certainly did not feel that I had failed. Quite to the contrary, but I *did* run out of time to fulfill my goal of increasing their client base, just as foreclosure activity began to rise once again. Despite having a couple of small potential clients nearer to signing up with the asset management company, we parted ways in February of 2011. I will always be grateful for the opportunity my friend gave me to re-enter the default servicing industry. It was a personally gratifying period in my life. I rapidly came to realize that it was far too soon to even "semi" retire. My successes at Great Western Bank, Washington Mutual and Citicorp Trust Bank were validated by the respect I received everywhere I traveled. As it turned out, our parting was another blessing in disguise, to say the least.

I received several potentially fulfilling and lucrative offers in the days and weeks since leaving the outsource company. This is in addition to authoring this book, which is another way for me to fulfill my responsibility to even greater numbers of individuals; as is giving my motivational presentation to various trade associations, corporations, organizations and schools across America... for the *right* reasons. Who knows what other opportunities lay ahead? I'm already planning to author additional books. Perhaps I'll return to radio? It is quite exhilarating just thinking about it. I welcome new challenges, as you clearly now know.

Every position I have held, all the knowledge and skills I have accumulated, the encouragement and inspiration of others I received, the experiences and successes, and, yes, failures, all of this and more have earned me many exciting opportunities. Thank You Lord!

My motivational speaking activities were greatly influenced in 1995 by encouragement I received in a personal letter from Zig Ziglar, the greatest inspirational speaker and trainer I have ever heard or whose motivational books I have read. In his letter to me he thanked me for sharing some of my experiences with him and said that he believed that my story could be inspirational and of encouragement to many people. I had seen Mr. Ziglar live in action more than once and have read several of his best-selling books. He was one of the catalysts, in fact, for my having authored this book. Another was Sarah Palin. Her personal character as the mother of a child with special needs influenced me to read her best-selling book, *Going Rogue*. She personally autographed it for me. The book was sent to me by one of her closest friends in Wasilla, Alaska, Kristan Cole. I had met Kristan's husband, Brad, at a default servicing conference in Dallas in September of 2010 (as you recall, I do not believe in coincidences or chance meetings). After reading Governor Palin's book I made a commitment to finally finish the book I had started to write over a decade ago.

I believe, as Zig Ziglar wrote in one of his many books, *Over the Top*, paraphrased here, that when you help other people get what they want, you will ultimately get what you want. He also said that no matter where you are in life, and what you may or may not have accomplished, from that moment on you must do all that you can to "finish well." I am now, and have been ever since I read those words in 1995, on a mission to finish well. Even though I will continue to work in other capacities, it is my motivational speaking activities that drive me today to accomplish this mission. The journey continues.

It is my deep abiding belief that all people are put on earth by God for a special purpose. Mine was revealed to me by Coach Ewing H. Crutchfield. He was a man I deeply admire because of what he did to reach out and help me to achieve my goals in high school, make me a better person, and lead me to my true calling; a man who told me while he was literally on his death bed in December of 2000 that I was the most determined athlete he had ever coached.

I do not regret having to navigate through life while negotiating the many challenges placed before me. Despite some struggles and setbacks I am a better person today because of it, just as my father so often said I would be. Some of these setbacks were self-created or self-inflicted in some cases; because of my desire to seek new challenges and career opportunities. I *do* regret some of the difficulties the traversing caused for my family. I cannot change the past, but I certainly apologize to them for having put them through such adversity, over which they had so little control. But I also hope that they have come to realize or soon will that I was *compelled* to follow the paths I have chosen to take. I was obligated to stretch beyond being comfortable. Beyond being average and past being timid or apprehensive about reaching for the stars and tenaciously grabbing for the brass ring; to be "in the arena." Winners never give up, and never give in. I never have, and I never will. Neither should you! That is the essence of perseverance and it is truly powerful.

It is my sincere, heartfelt expectation that those who have read this book have come to realize that you have the power within you to achieve greater success than you may have otherwise believed. That you will take away the lesson that the "secret" to success is that there is no secret — it is simply the combination of hard work, sacrifice, a burning desire to achieve your boldly stated goals, flexibility and steel determination that empower you to persevere despite any obstacles in your path.

An ordinary person can achieve extraordinary goals. I am living proof of that. Being "different" is good; so is competition and fierce determination to overcome adversity to achieve success. Has it been a wild ride? Yes, but it has been a ride I would not change. I am excited about the future and what it may hold. As God is my witness, I am as determined as ever to continue to fulfill my "Responsibility." **Believe to Achieve.**

Afterword

It is no surprise to many of us who knew Lynn and played football with him that he would be a successful adult in his pursuits after high school. What we didn't know was the incredible influence he would have on so many other people or that he would remain so inspiring for more than 40 years following our graduation in 1968.

Having known Lynn since elementary school, it is no wonder that his words throughout this book should be both challenging and inspiring. The common themes that emerge from playing football; hard work, dedication, sacrifice, and teamwork – have defined Lynn to this day. If nothing else, Lynn's words provide personal guidance and inspiration for anyone who wants to achieve beyond what is normally perceived by others as unachievable.

As teammates of Lynn at Wilson, we all knew him simply as a hard-working, dedicated Wilson High School football player – part of our "team" and an important cog in our dream of winning the championship our senior year. I found out while reading this book that his personal goals were very much woven into how our own team created a stunning victory over near defeat.

We all understood the importance of tradition here at Wilson where I have been teaching for many years, and how competitive it would be to not only achieve success on the football field, but also in classrooms and in life. We were fortunate to have had the skilled guidance of coaches who were also respected educators, many of whom had been in the military. We all felt like sons to these men because they were also thoughtful and caring; sometimes harsh, yet fair, role models. Lynn's own family strength lent itself to what we achieved as a football team

Lynn is no "Superman" and didn't possess any hidden powers when he was a student-athlete at Wilson. He was in fact, an "everyman" in the sense that he knew how much work it would take to even just make the team, and then to actually play! He was also a typical teenager who often acted humorously and spontaneously. We spent many summer hours together fooling around and sailing his and his brother's Lido 14 in Alamitos Bay, as well as sweating it out on the football field. His likeability and well-roundedness is evident today as he no doubt has countless friends that have simply enjoyed him beyond Lynn Effinger the housing industry executive and inspirational speaker.

As Lynn hinted within these pages, there is also no "secret" to achieving success since everything he has accomplished is achievable for us all within the human spirit. Countless stories have been told about how people overcome challenges. But in Lynn's case, there was really nothing to overcome! Like the blind person who doesn't need sight, or the cancer victim who doesn't submit to his disease, Lynn simply lives his life and continues to challenge every day as if it is fourth down and a yard to go for a game-winning touchdown!

–Wes Edwards

Acknowledgements

THERE ARE A NUMBER OF special people who I would like to thank for their support over the years and the many who helped encourage me to put into book form these reflections in *Believe to Achieve – The Power of Perseverance*. First and foremost is my wife Kathy. My children know full well how much she deserves special thanks and far more for having made the commitment to me in 1970 to share our lives together, for better or for worse. It has been both, of course, but the "better" has been wonderful. While Kathy has been one of my most vocal cheerleaders when warranted, she has been equally vociferous in her criticism, when she felt it necessary. I am grateful to her for both and my deep love for her is infinite. She deserves much more than I can ever repay her.

My children, Scott, Diana and Chris have shared the good, the bad and the ugly but have never wavered in their love and support. We have shared many, many great times over the years and some tears as well. I love them all dearly, each in a distinct way, yet the same. But I should also apologize to each of them, especially Scotty, for being my pre-technology "remote control" for the television. Each of our children performed this function, albeit begrudgingly, and I want them to know I appreciated their efforts as much or more than my mostly weekend laziness on the couch.

I also want to thank my mother's late parents, Robert and Cora Bidwell, for always being so kind to me, loving me and being such wonderful story-book grandparents. I miss you both tremendously. And Doyle, my mother's younger brother who was and is a great (and cool) human being, as is his loving wife, Bess.

I have been blessed to have had many coaches, teachers, mentors and friends over the years. I will thank many here but if I leave anyone off the following list of people I admire and to whom I wish to express gratitude for their guidance, friendship and support, I humbly apologize: My Little League Baseball Coach, Lonnie; Alan Kinnard; my favorite elementary school teachers; Mrs. Bacon and Mrs. Winslow; my long-time friends, Wes Edwards, Patti Gehrke, and Monica Cosenza; my favorite junior high school teachers; Mrs. Milkes and Coach Hasson; high school coaches; Russell Jordan, John Morton, Owen Dixon and Skip Rowland; my close friend of many years in school, the late Jim Pollock. My teammates; Dennis Dummit, Jeff Severson, Jim Creighton, Jim Hunt, Greg Sears, Kent Eastman, Randy Stein, Mark Lewis, Randy Rossi, Dick Burdge, Jeff Burroughs, Chris Key, Steve Corwin, Ed Giles, Paul Eddy, Charlie Shaw and so many other great guys. The late Hank Hollingworth, Bob Flowers, Coach Williams, Frank Higgins, the late George Kelly and Miles Davidson, the late, great, Mr. Nathan Shapell, John Haltom, Mark Bragg, Sue McNalley, Dave Gibson, Amy Bitz, Brad Wachsmuth, Marianna Fowles, Alice Sullivan, Shelley Kaye, Teri Workman, and, of course, Ted Marchibroda and the late Coach George Allen. I also want to thank Van Barbieri for introducing me to Etty Allen,

Coach Allen's wife of so many years and for securing several speaking opportunities for me, including one at the NFL Alumni of Greater Los Angeles. Also, special thanks to Van Barbieri and Kiersten Allen, Coach George Allen's daughter-in-law for inviting Kathy and me to the special celebration in Canton, Ohio in 2002 following the induction of Coach Allen into the Pro Football Hall of Fame. That was a tremendous thrill and a high honor, indeed.

It is also important that I acknowledge the help that my mother-in-law, Ellen Knauff, who passed away just one month before her 77th birthday in 2010, was to Kathy and me during the early years of our marriage; including helping us with much of the down payment on our first home. She was a kind-hearted woman who had more than her share of difficulties and disappointments in her life, but her kindness to me and our family in those early years is not forgotten, nor unappreciated.

Special thanks also must be given to Patty Galloway, Kathy's only sister. I have known her for over forty-two years and she has been such an important part of my life, although not as much as she has been to Kathy's. Patty is one of those most rare individuals, like her sister, who consistently put the needs of others far ahead of her own. She is a remarkably strong, caring and resilient woman who I respect almost as much as her older sister. I love you Patty, and always will.

Another person (and her family) that must be acknowledged here, for a variety of reasons, is Evangeline "Vangie" Valenzuela-Nadig. Vangie has been my wife's closest friend since they were both 13 years old. They are in many ways closer than me and Kathy (drat!). But Vangie and her husband, Rudy Nadig are good friends of ours who have shared many good times with us over the years. Vangie is part of an incredibly close family that I admire beyond words. When I am long gone I know in my heart that Kathy and Vangie will continue their wonderful friendship forever.

I also want to again acknowledge to the world that I am blessed to have four incredible, smart and loving grandchildren: Payton, Tanner, Ian and Holly. All of whom have given me such tremendous joy and happiness. I only wish I could see them all more often.

To my much older brother, Kirk (just kidding), my younger brother Brian, and my sister, Valerie, I also want to thank you for your love over the years, even when I may not have deserved it.

To my parents, Bill Effinger and Shirley Lulay, there are no adequate words to thank you enough for everything you have done for me over the years; providing a loving home life, teaching me right from wrong, exposing me to the Catholic Church, instilling in me a strong work ethic and empathy for others. Thank you also for praising me when I deserved it and scolding me as I deserved that as well, but particularly for inculcating deep within me a belief that I could achieve anything I really wanted to. And for the encouragement you have always given me in my athletic endeavors, family life and vocational career (especially Dad for helping me with my career so many times), as well as my motivational speaking activities. Thank you both, as well as Diana Frye-Effinger, my father's wife, for your detailed help in editing my manuscript.

I also want to publicly thank Bob Zachmeier, an incredibly successful real estate broker, author in his own right and personal friend, for unselfishly editing the almost final draft of my book despite the tremendous demands on his time from so many quarters. Bob, you are the BEST!

Thank you also Lia Ladas for your help and encouragement with this project. Your expertise and empathy for helping me share my personal story is deeply appreciated.

Special thanks also to one of my heroes, Zig Ziglar, for being such a tremendous influence on my motivational speaking activities and for allowing me to quote him from the letter he sent to me in July of 1995 that appears on the back cover of this book.

I also must thank The Honorable George Allen, Former Governor and Senator from Virginia, and my longtime friend, George Chamberlin for agreeing to allow me to put their quotes about this book on its back cover. It means a great deal to me to have their endorsements.

Thanks are also in order to Matt Luke for contributing his special, kind and generous thoughts in this book's Foreword. Matt has an incredible life story of his own and understands intimately some of the things I went through while growing up. And to my longtime friend, Wes Edwards for writing the Afterword, thank you from the bottom of my heart. I admire you both and look forward to continuing our friendship in the future.

I also want to thank every teacher, administrator, coach and fellow student at Long Beach Woodrow Wilson High School through the years for being a part of my life, known or unknown; a life that no doubt benefitted in the extreme from the traditions, high educational standards, and focus on ethics and integrity that was instilled in us all. *Hail to Wilson!*

My great friend, Patti Gehrke, deserves very special thanks for taking the time to meticulously edit the final proof of this book. This was beyond the call of duty, but very much appreciated.

I would be remiss in the extreme if I did not also thank the wonderful people at CreateSpace, especially those on Project Team 2, for all their professional, timely and valuable assistance in publishing this book. I could not be more pleased about your high level of customer service, talent and hard work.

While I have already called significant attention to why I admire Coach Crutchfield so much and thank him for his belief in my ability to help others to overcome adversity to be the best they can be, I could not possibly leave him out of this acknowledgement. God Bless you Coach, God Bless my friends and family… and God Bless America. In no other country could someone like me achieve the level of success I have enjoyed in so many wide-ranging aspects of my life.

Lynn Effinger
May 18, 2011

About the Author

LYNN EFFINGER IS A VETERAN of nearly four decades within the housing and mortgage default servicing industries, having served as Vice President-REO Manager for Great Western Bank, Washington Mutual and Citicorp Trust Bank, as well as Director of Advertising and Public Relations for Shapell Industries, Inc. and Great Western Real Estate. He has also served as a marketing consultant to builders, developers, real estate companies and mortgage lenders throughout Southern California, and Director of REO Services for Safeguard Properties, Inc. Lynn is the former Producer and Host of *Real Estate Matters*, a weekly radio talk show in San Diego, California, and the former Editor and Publisher of *Escondido* magazine. He is the author of numerous articles relating to the housing and default servicing industries, marketing, personal performance and political commentaries that have been published over the years in a variety of trade publications, magazines and local newspapers. He is a frequent guest speaker and expert panelist at various mortgage default servicing industry conferences, meetings and seminars and is the President of Effinger Communications. Lynn is an accomplished motivational speaker, trainer and mentor who believes deeply in community service, charitable giving and volunteerism. He is making every effort to spread his message not only to corporations, trade associations and other business and civic organizations, but also to high schools and colleges around the country. Lynn Effinger currently resides in Temecula, California with his wife and best friend of forty-one years, Kathy.

To book Lynn Effinger to motivate and inspire your sales team, students, trade association, civic club, or other organization, please visit his web site at www.effingercommunications.com

Made in the USA
Charleston, SC
04 September 2011